I0160454

Presented To:

_____

From:

_____

Date:

_____

BUILT TO PROSPER

Built To Prosper

The 9 Principles of Self Mastery

Hasheem Francis

BTP
Publishing Group
WHERE LEADERS HAVE A VOICE

Plymouth, FL

For information about reprints rights, translation, or bulk purchases, please contact Deborah Francis at **info@BTPPublish.com** or you can write to BTP Publishing, LLC, and P.O Box 552, Plymouth, FL 32768. **www.HasheemFrancis.com**

Built To Prosper The 9 Principles of Self Mastery
Cover designed by: BTP Marketing Group, LLC.
Edited By: BTP Marketing Group, LLC.
ISBN: 9780983555452
Published by: BTP Publishing Group. Plymouth, FL

BUILT TO PROSPER

DEDICATION

To my wife Deborah, whose love and support means more than words can express. To my lovely daughters India and Savannah, your tender hugs give me the strength to move mountains. Also to the next and future generation, may the thoughts in this book inspire you to achieve greatness.

BUILT TO PROSPER

CONTENTS

BUILT TO PROSPER

BUILT TO PROSPER
MENTORING
BUSINESS AND LEADERSHIP DEVELOPMENT

"Be a great student of life, so you can be an outstanding teacher of living." **Hasheem Francis**

Mentors Help YOU Excel To The Next Level! It is a fact that most people who mentor do it because they LOVE helping others! They love working with someone and helping him get from where he is to where he wants to be, bringing out his best, helping him think bigger, fostering those big breakthroughs, etc.

Built To Prosper Mentoring Program remains the most comprehensive program of its kind and a leader's best choice for exceeding his maximum goals. If you are highly motivated and want the individualized or corporate mentoring by one of our true experts, then you need our mentoring program. Our mentors specialize in giving you the latest techniques on how to build a profitable business, become an effective leader, amass wealth, and develop a healthy lifestyle. Your mentor will also instruct you on the most effective use of our proprietary materials and techniques. Built To Prosper Mentoring focuses on four areas: Business, Leadership, Wealth, and Health. Mentoring enables you to reach your full potential in life and gives you the ability to promote your personal and professional development in a strategic and supportive way, leading to enhanced returns on your investment.

Visit us at: www.BTPMentoring.com

ACKNOWLEDGMENTS

Many have helped influence this body of work. I am deeply grateful for every person who has inspired and encouraged me through their written word or through their presence.

I would like to acknowledge and express my gratitude to all the mentors, past and present teachers, business partners, friends, and family members who have guided me throughout my journey.

Special thanks to all those who have shared their God-given gifts with the world: Dr. Leroy Thompson, Creflo Dollar, Jesse Duplantis, Kenneth Copeland, Bob Proctor, Kenneth Estrada, John C. Maxwell, Bob Harrison, Anthony Robbins, Darren Hardy, Oprah Winfrey, Richard Branson, Nick Nicholas, Robert Kiyosaki, Kim Kiyosaki, Harold Herring, Bishop E. Bernard Jordan, Rev Ike, Napoleon Hill, Bruce Wilkinson, TD Jakes, Jeff Olson, Robert Allen, Mark Victor Hansen, Jack Canfield, Catherine Ponder, Sharon Lechter, Wallace Wattles, Barack Obama, Zig Ziglar, Paul J. Meyer, Stephen R. Covey, Jim Stovall, Norman Vincent Peal, Dr. Joseph Murphy, Og Magdino, Joyce Meyer, Denis Waitley, Brian Tracy, Jim Rohn, Charlie T. Jones, Nido Qubein.

Thanks to the following organizations who develop the resources that help others achieve greatness: Ever Increasing Word Ministries, Cashology Academy, Built To Prosper University, The Nightingale and Conant Company, The Rich Dad Company, Built To Prosper Magazine, Millionaire University, Enlightened Wealth Institute, Rich Life Investments, LLC., The Napoleon Hill Foundation, Success Inc., Life Success Productions, The Joy of Healthy Living, Pay Your Family First, Dale Carnegie Training, SelfGrowth.com, Debt Free Army, INJOY, The John Maxwell Company, Robins Research International Inc., Franklin Covey, and The Ken Blanchard Companies.

INTRODUCTION

> **"Empowerment is what gets you started. Purpose is what keeps you focused. Commitment is what get the job done. It's better to start than to live a life of regrets"**
> **Hasheem Francis**

I would like to commend you for investing in yourself. In this wonderful experience we call life, you reap what you sow. This book is a complete guide on building the life you truly desire. I know that is a bold claim to make; and the only way to know if these claims are true is by results. Most of my life, I have studied many personal development systems and applied the success principles to get the results I desired.

What I have found, and my mentor expressed this to me a million times, is **success leaves clues.** You may be wondering why it took me so long to understand this insight. Like most people I thought I knew it all. It was when I became coachable that I began to understand and apply the principles of success. I discovered that prosperity is not just about financial blessings. It also includes peace, wisdom, favor, success, good health, and every good thing you could possibly need—all the wonderful things God desires for you to have. **God's will is for you to prosper in spirit, soul and body.** Author Napoleon Hill stated; "No one is ready for a thing until he believes he can acquire it."

It took some time before I saw the result I desired in my life; it was not an overnight success. I was willing to go through the process no matter how long it was going to take. That said, I want you to be fully aware that it is going to take time and **you must be committed to the**

process. Success does not happen overnight, but it can happen for anyone who is willing to make focused plans, be committed to the process, and never give up.

Who decides whether you will be successful or not? (Cue the "Jeopardy" theme music) The final answer: **YOU do**! In order to prosper and succeed, you must first have the desire to do so and be willing to stay the course. You are the captain of your results. On this journey, I will be your coach. You may not like everything I ask you to do, but you will appreciate it later when you see the results. If you are going to have a life-changing experience, you must participate in the process.

I promise you, I will give you the principles and strategies, and the only requirement I have as your coach is that you take full responsibility for the results and be committed to the process.

I say this because time and time again, I have seen many people start on this journey of personal growth and development and if they do not get the results overnight, they blame everyone under the sun. The truth is, this person decided not to be committed; they wanted a quick fix. Or on the other hand, there is the person that will achieve some sort of success, and then say it was all their brilliance that made them successful. As time go on, their ego gets in the way and they stop doing the things that got them the results. I want you to go all the way; I want you to develop yourself to the point where the principles in this book actually become a habit for you.

When I started on the success journey I had to get my stinking thinking out the way so a new way of thinking could be developed. It took some time to develop this new prosperous way of thinking because I had some deep-rooted erroneous beliefs to get rid of. I played the victim game and blamed everyone under the sun for the unfavorable circumstances in my life. I blamed my parents, the school system, the government, and my siblings. I even blamed the seven dogs that chased me back in the eighth grade when I was going to the school dance.

(Pardon me, I had a flashback moment.)

To get what I desired in life, I had to go through a total transformation, a complete change in my mind about some of the things I believed to be true, and honestly, it was quite a struggle. When you have been raised with beliefs that were passed down for generations then wake up one day and learn those beliefs have been keeping you back, it is a fight to change. Change is difficult when you are not willing to give up a counter-productive belief. Many are not willing to change and that is why they will continue to get the same results time after time. **To make real changes in our lives, we must first be prepared to take responsibility for ourselves and our choices.**

There is nothing satisfying or rewarding in living in a constant state of lack. I have seen both sides of lack and wealth. I know what it is like not to have and I know what it is like to experience more than enough, and I must truly say I enjoy living an abundant life. When I speak about abundance, I am talking about all areas of life: faith, mental, health, family, relationships, business/career, and finances.

All true success is personally defined. You decide the goal, the pace and the parameters around which you are willing to be successful. You have only you to please in your success. You create your world by the way you think. Nothing in your world has any meaning except the meaning you assign by how you think and feel about it. Where your mind goes, creative energy flows. In order for you to become prosperous, you must think in a different order of magnitude from those who are content with just getting by.

Are you where you want to be? Do you feel healthy? Are your relationships as you would like them to be? Are you financially secure?

There are no limits to attaining your most desired hopes and goals as long as you can define what it is you want to achieve in life. A great deal of what you have perceived as limits in your life are actually limits you have placed upon yourself. The good news is you have already begun to eliminate them. You began the very moment you picked up this book, which will help you address them directly. Many people today do not know what they want, and they do not have any direction for their lives. Someone once said to me, and I still reflect on this insight constantly, "Do not die with your music left inside of you, be all that God created you to be. Be more, do more, and have more."
Breaking the curse of procrastination is a battle that has to be fought and won mentally, physically, and spiritually. This infirmity has delayed many people's destinies, including myself, for many years. Loosening its stubborn grip on my life was not easy. I formed destructive habits that were the results of the stinking thinking about myself and those around me. I had to change the do-nothing-but-want-something attitude and take responsibility for how my life turned out. I had to pay the full retail price for success. Was it worth it? Absolutely!

I realized God created me in His image and wealth was His will for me. God did not predetermine who would be prosperous or who would live in lack. He simply created His spiritual laws, and freely gave them to everyone. Every person then has a choice to implement the laws of prosperity or the laws of scarcity.

I had what you would call an awakening, the day of reckoning. I was not going to accept the lifestyle "I" created with my thoughts and actions. This was the day I took back my power, and accepted responsibility for the mess I created. I became aware of who I was, who I belonged to, and what was promised to me. I realized that the life we each live is the life within the limits of our own thinking.

I sought out the truth about wealth and its availability to me. It was always there for my enjoyment, but I could not recognize it. It is like when you hear someone say, "I will be happy when." It was not the stuff that was going to make me happy, it was freedom from scarcity. When I say freedom from scarcity, I am not just speaking in terms of finances; I am talking about a form of thinking. Poverty is a mindset that creates unfavorable circumstances in all areas of your life. You know that everyone who has really prospered or reached an exceptional level of success has one thing in common: they have broken the bondage of their limitations.

> "It takes courage to go your own way, ignoring the crowd and the critics opinion. The more challenges you conquer, the more YOU can conquer. " Hasheem Francis

It was when I took an honest look at my life and the results I was getting that I came to a moment of truth: I was not happy with the results. I wanted more. I desired to have meaningful relationships; I desired a healthy body, a body that, when I looked in the mirror, I could smile and say, "You look good." I desired the financial ability to provide for my family and be a blessing to others. I understood that I had to expand my prosperity consciousness in order to break out of a scarcity mentality.

When I took responsibility for the circumstances of my life, I acknowledged that I created them. I could either take responsibility or play the victim game. I realized that if I chose the victim position, I lost power. If I chose responsibility, then I had the power to do something about my circumstances. The more responsibility I accepted for the consequences of my actions, the more power I assumed.

I began to change my thinking, my belief, and my environment. I learned how to let go of negative people, places, and things that did not add value to my life. My character and future began to be molded by my thoughts, actions, and associations. I became aware of prosperity and unlimited opportunities that were available to me.

Prosperity began to demonstrate itself in my life in many ways, for which I am truly grateful. It started with gaining an understanding of my relationship with GOD. I am not here to convert you to any religious belief, because that is a personal journey. I just applied the spiritual teachings that I received and got results in my life. I learned to accept me and love myself and others. I am blessed with a wonderful family who loves me for me, and I have wonderful relationships all across the country. On the business side, I doubled my income for the past ten years. My family and I have traveled to so many different places it became difficult to keep track of it all. I had to hire an assistant to schedule our trips.

I have used the principles in this book to achieve more than I ever dreamed, imagined, or desired. I have found what is truly important in life and am in awe of the unlimited possibilities that still lie ahead. This is not just for me or a select few, the same is going to happen for you as you apply these principles. My desire is for you to develop a success consciousness that cannot be taken away. You deserve to be successful. It is not for a chosen few, it is for everyone who desires it and applies the correct principles.

I truly believe God showed me the way so I can teach others and show that God does not have favorites, and what He has done for me and many others, He can and will definitely do for you. What I learned I would love to share with everyone who has a desire to be more, do more and have more. You were created in God's image, so everything you need you already have. God gave each of us the ability to get wealth, but the ability He gave us must be utilized in order to receive it.

The tools within YOU must be cultivated and applied properly to achieve the life you desire.

If it is change you seek, like having loving and fun relationships or control over your life, you must break free from all self-destructive habits, conditioning, and thinking, and then adopt a complete surrender to prosperous thinking. You must develop a wealth consciousness. It is impossible to achieve real success otherwise.

There will come an important moment in your life when you discover for yourself the great mystery of life: That things may happen to you, and things may happen around you, but the only thing that really matters is what happens in you. There is an abundance of resources and mentors who have paved the way and left a road map for you to follow to achieve your goals.

As we embark on this journey, you must ask yourself, "What do I want out of life?" Many people live their lives without ever asking this important question. As a result, their lives become a series of events dictated by external circumstances instead of inner needs and desires. Unless you know what your desires are, you have no choice but to bounce from one activity to another, looking for a quick fix, forced to accept whatever comes your way.

This book is meant to challenge you into actively pursuing a new level of wealth consciousness by understanding and applying these concepts in your life. You will not grasp the message in this book unless you read and apply it with an open mind. Wealth is everywhere, become aware of endless opportunities that surround you. **You are Built To Prosper!**

This is Your Personal Book.

Insert your name, it is your destiny:

I know the plans I have for you

(   ) declares the Lord,
plans to prosper you (   ) and not
to harm you (   ) plans to
give you (   ) hope and a
future. Jeremiah 29:11

THE FOUNDATION

> "The character ethic, which I believe to be the foundation of success, teaches that there are basic principles of effective living, and that people can only experience true success and enduring happiness as they learn and integrate these principles into their basic character." Stephen R. Covey

One of the requirements in reading and understanding a map is that you have to know exactly where you are before you can figure out where you are going. And that is precisely what I have purposed to do here. I want to help you locate yourself. You cannot be a quitter on this journey; you have to consistently do what you know to do. **Are you ready for change?** Are you willing to develop yourself until you break free from the bondage of defeat? It is going to take effort on your part, and I am going to do mine: provide you with all the tools you need to help you become all that you desire. However, it is up to you to pick the tools up and use them.

Very few are aware of the true meaning of life, of what is really worthwhile, and what it is to know oneself. Only those who know themselves can succeed. Your life means something. You may not have found that meaning yet, but you will. For you to be prosperous, you will have to deliberately choose to be. Choice is the means and the end. Your prosperity will come from your choices in the way you use your mind. You have a reason to prosper; you have a purpose beyond what you think. You were not put on this earth to live an average life and just get by; you are to live life to the maximum.

You must give yourself permission to be wealthy. You are created to expand, it is natural. Wanting is how you grow. You are not selfish or greedy when you desire the best for your life, you are stretching to realize your greatest potential. Many people are not willing to do what is necessary to reach their fullest potential and that is why they will go to their graves with regrets. Many push their purpose and dreams aside for a paycheck or make excuses about not having enough time to do what they know in their heart is the right thing to do. Life is about more understanding, more wisdom, more love, more laughter, more rain, more sunshine, more giving, more receiving. We are to be a blessing to others while we are here, and the only way to be a blessing is to be blessed ourselves. It is only right that you live a life of success and victory.

Rather than allowing others to define success for you, take the time today to create your own definition. Have the courage to measure your success by standards that are meaningful for your life. How do you define success? What does success look like to you? Take a few moments and think about these questions. Only you can answer them, because success is personal.

_____

_____

_____

_____

_____

_____

_____

_____

_____

_____

_____

_____

_____

_____

_____

_____

_____

Many equate success with money and material wealth. Even though these things can be an outward sign of your own career or business success or that of your family, it reflects only a small piece of the bigger picture that is your life. The principles described in this book are about you becoming all that God designed you to be. There must be a conscious effort on your part to learn the necessary principles and obtain what you need to be prosperous. I know you are on the right track. You invested in yourself by purchasing this book, and once again I commend you. **You are a student of the game of life**.

You are going to learn how to live and work from the inside. When you live from the inside, the outside circumstances must fall into place. Nothing in this world can stop you but you. Knowing and applying the principles of success will set you free from the bondage of lack, want, and poverty. To perform at your best, you need to know who you are and why you think and feel the way you do. It is only when you understand and accept yourself that you can begin moving forward in other areas of your life. A successful life should encompass far more than your work or finances, although they are a part of the big picture. A fulfilling life in all areas is a successful life.

> **"You are the writer of your life story, you are the director of your life movie." Rhonda Byrne**

Life is what you make it, so why not make your life a prosperous one? We live in an ever increasing universe filled with abundance. We were created by The Creator who is available to fulfill our every need and desire. It is our divine nature to want more and to gravitate towards abundance. Every person naturally wants to be wealthy, to be and have all that he or she is capable of being and having. We were created to manifest good on this earth.

On some level everyone wants a life filled with an abundance of love, joy, happiness, health, wonderful relationships, peace, and we can not forget money. Are you going where you want to go, doing what you want to do, and becoming who you want to become? The law of attraction says that what you focus on with your consciousness will be manifest in your experience of reality. The attractive power of any particular thought is determined by how often you have that thought and by the strength of the feelings or emotions associated with it. The more energy you give to a particular thought, the greater its power to attract its corresponding circumstance into your physical world. Therefore, whether you focus on what you desire or do not desire, you will experience more of those things you focus on.

It is natural to want the best for you and your family, the best foods for your body (which is your temple), the best clothing, and the most comfortable home filled with all the amenities you desire. Living prosperous is Godly; you become blessed, to be a blessing to others. You can decide to become prosperous and God will cheerfully provide. Opportunities and blessings come to the person who embraces a prosperous attitude. Others have created the life of their dreams. So can you.

Creating a prosperous life comes with a price and only those who are willing to pay that price will become prosperous. You may be thinking, "What is the price must I pay?" You have to change the old negative images, and habits of how you think, talk, and feel about wealth. **You must claim your birthright: the rich life**. Will it be an easy task? Absolutely not! You may be saying, "Hey, wait a minute, I bought this book so I can get rich quick. I want my success today, as a matter fact I want my success now." I understand, I have been there before, I had that same attitude at one point and it got me nowhere. Some so-called "gurus" may tell you that you can quantum leap to success, but my friend, it just does not work that way. It requires work and 90% of the work is on your thinking, beliefs, and attitude.

Many people today give up because they are not committed to the process of developing themselves. Due to their lack of commitment, they settle for what life gives them. But you, my friend, I desire the best for you and you will receive it only if you believe and stay committed to the process. We are apt to think of people who have been successful in life and in business as being greatly favored by fortune and we account for it in all sorts of ways but the right one. The truth is their success represents their expectation of themselves, the sum of their creative, habitual thinking. Their mental attitude has manifested and created their reality. They have created what they have and what they are out of their constructive thought and their unquenchable faith in the Higher Power and themselves.

We must not only believe we can succeed, but we must believe with all our heart. Our life manifests from our most dominant thoughts and feelings. Just as whatever we plant grows, that which we focus our attention multiplies. You are the fruit of the thoughts you have planted and nourished. If you want a better harvest, you must plant better thoughts. Whatever we put in our minds comes out in our lives. We select the circumstances that occur in our lives by choosing how and where we focus our attention. Every negative thought has a consequence. If you want success, then you must have successful thoughts and have a positive conviction that you will attain success.

> "I've come to believe that all my past failure and frustrations were actually laying the foundation for the understandings that have created the new level of living I now enjoy." Anthony Robbins

Poverty is a curse, which has and continues to destroy many. Holding on to scarcity thoughts will continue to create scarcity-producing conditions. Poor thoughts will not produce prosperity. Many are unaware of the abundance that is available to them; some believe they do not deserve to have wealth; then there are those who may believe that to deny oneself of wealth is noble. There is nothing noble about living in lack, not knowing how you are going to pay the bills, or feed your family. Go tell a man who needs to provide for his family that it is noble for his children to be hungry. Make sure you run after you make that statement.

I believe some people use the wealth denial factor as an excuse to not use their God-given ability. Who wants to be a person who pays their bills late, receives handouts from others, or is always owing and not owning? The individual who persists in holding their mental attitude towards poverty, or is always thinking of their hard luck and failure to succeed, can by no possibility go in the opposite direction, where the goal of prosperity lies.

> **"The rich ruleth over the poor, and the borrower is servant to the lender." Proverbs 22:7, KJV**

That is why most lenders love to loan money to you. You become their servant, and they become your master. Are you hoping for greater health, wealth, love, and success? The time has come for you to **'Owe no man anything, but to love one another." (Roman 13:6)**

The time is now; the harvest has come. You shall reap the abundance you desire if you have faith and believe that there is more than enough. There is a time when the possible and the prosperous spirit in you are going to meet and manifest your desires. You should always desire that which is good for you and your family. To seek a better life, you first have to decide what you want for your life. If you learn to take responsibility for your life, you will come to an understanding that you are where you are today because of the decisions you have made. A decision that you can make today is that you will do what it takes to develop a wealthy mindset.

Simply wishing for a better life is insufficient. If anyone is to make any steps towards their definite objectives, then they need to have a determined attitude, bordering on obsession, to fulfill that desire. It does not matter what you desire. It may be a desire to excel in business or to be a better person in your relationships, or it could be to take better care of your health. As soon as you empower yourself to prosper and overcome any fears of failure and success, you will realize that you deserve all that you desire, and move towards what you want, rather than towards what you do not want. You are consciously making the decision to win in life.

Think big about life, have faith that whatever you desire will come to you if you remain persistent and consistent in acting on your vision. This is not one of those books where you are filled with affirmations and then expect abundance to fall in your lap while you are sitting at home watching T.V.

There is nothing wrong with declaring affirmations, but some action must be taken afterwards. From the words of one of my favorite authors, Shaam S-Dot Jones: *"Recognize, plan, and then do something."*

Why is it that people in our society lead lives of quiet desperation? Less than 10%, and I am being modest, achieve real success in life. We live in a world that provides the most opportunity to be prosperous, achieve financial success, and live a life of fulfillment.

In today's society many expect the worst. If you need proof, take me up on this challenge: When you get in your office in the morning, go to the nearest water cooler, coffee maker, or even get in the elevator with someone on a Monday morning, and you will hear so much negative talk it could literally drive you insane. Many are concerned about their job, what people think about them, how they are going to pay the bills, and constantly complaining about their spouse with people who do not need to know their personal business. I call these people energy drainers. They bring rain to the picnic. Most people are comfortable with negativity, and you can never make changes when you are comfortable. A wise mentor once told me, "Success is outside of your comfort zone."

In order to create a life filled with prosperity and wealth we need to become aware of what paradigm we are functioning from, either prosperity or a scarcity mentality. One way to find out is by asking yourself, "Am I willing to help others?" Those that function from a prosperity mindset are always looking for an opportunity to give. Those that function from a scarcity mentality think that when they give, they are losing. Business philosopher Bob Proctor states, "Givers always gain."

Develop the expectation that great things will happen out of the ordinary. Think about wealth, and open yourself up to the unlimited flow of good. You must think prosperity, see prosperity, feel prosperity, believe prosperity and most importantly experience prosperity. **Let no thought of limitation enter your mind.**

> **"Don't judge yourself by others' standards – develop your own. Don't get caught up in the trap of changing yourself to fit the world. The world has to change to fit YOU." Hasheem Francis**

How do you determine your self-worth? By money, good looks, education, fine clothes, an executive office, or a luxury automobile? When someone has a low self image, they sometimes try to compensate for these feelings by trying to increase their value through the attainment of material things or by condemning those who have achieved success.

In developing your foundation of being prosperous you must develop a strong sense of self-worth without the attachment to material things.

To be truly happy, you need a clear sense of direction. You need to feel that your life stands for something, that you are somehow making a valuable contribution to your world.

There is nothing wrong with having expensive things in life; I enjoy opulence, but my self-worth is not tied to my accumulation of material wealth. My true wealth is the inner me and no one can take that away. I do not need permission or validation from anybody to be wealthy. Many people think wealth has to be based on achievements or material.

Wealth comes from the inside; no one can give it to you, just like I can not give you a body that is fit—I can not go into the gym for you and pump the weights and do all the cardio exercises for you. It is all up to you, that is your responsibility. I know many may desire a quick fix to increase their prosperity, but developing wealth is an inner process.

What is money really? Have you ever heard someone say money is not everything?

Money is a tool and a resource. Someone once told me, "money is not everything." My reply was, "Go tell your mortgage and credit card company that." Many people make having money a morality statement when it is neither moral nor immoral. Money itself is neither good nor evil. It has the ability to do only what its owner wants it to do. The owner is in charge. If you need proof, place a $100 bill on the table and see if it jumps up and does some evil. Waiting…waiting... Nothing yet? In all my years on this earth, Benjamin Franklin never forced me into doing something outside of my will. Money has no power in itself, but having control over how it will be used gives us power. Money serves its owner without question; it is ready to do good or evil at its owner's discretion.

Begin to view money as any other tool you have available for your use. How you use that tool will determine whether or not it does harm or good. Cars, ink, paper, hammer, nails, gasoline, airplanes, guns, money—all these can improve the quality of a person's life. However, all of them can cause severe harm when misused. You may be asking, "How can ink and paper cause severe harm if misused?" Have you written or read a story about someone that was degrading or making a claim against their character? They say the pen is mightier than the sword. The blessing or harm to your life is determined by whether or not these tools are wisely operated under your control. You are in danger when money begins to rule you, instead of you ruling it. If you are staying up all night tossing and turning, thinking about how you are going to get money to pay your bills, money and bills just became your master. Here is my recommendation: drink some hot chocolate and go to sleep.

In order to handle large amounts of money, you must be prepared. If you need proof, research those that have won the lottery—they end up worse off than before they won. Why? They were not mentally prepared. They received a large amount of money, but had a scarcity mentality. The more money we have, the more power we have. Money can control you if you do not have the right mindset for it. That is why most people will expect or depend on the government to take care of them. They never develop the proper philosophy of saving and investing their money; they have the paycheck-to-paycheck mentality.

Achieving your financial freedom is one of the most important goals and responsibilities of your life. A feeling of freedom is essential to the achievement of any other important goal, and you cannot be free until and unless you have enough money so that you are no longer preoccupied with it. When you decide exactly what you want and what your financial picture will look like, you will be able to achieve your goals faster than you might have imagined possible.

Money should never be hoarded; money is made to be circulated. You read so many tragic stories about people who die each year in poverty with their life savings stuffed in their favorite teddy bear. I recall reading a story that was written by business philosopher Bob Proctor in his *New York Times* bestselling book, *You Were Born Rich*. There was a story about a man who lived like a pauper. He collected cans around the neighborhood, and when he died, they found $100,000 in cash in his closet. There are probably a million more stories like this. What if he would have invested that money?

The key and secret about money is, the more you receive, the more you give, and the more you give, the more you will receive. It is the law.

If you want the same results as wealthy people, then you must take the necessary actions to create those results. Those that succeed in life commit to doing what they love and money will follow. When you are out working two and three jobs, you have reversed the role and became a servant to money. Another example of becoming a servant to money is when you work a job that you are not happy with and stay because of the money. You are working hard for the money, when your money should be working hard for you twenty-four hours a day.

Instead of becoming a slave to money or material things, you can make money serve you by developing a positive, appreciative attitude towards it. It is important to learn how to master money rather than be enslaved by it. Money is a good tool, if used properly. Learn to regard it as a servant that comes to help and assist your life for good living. You must shift your thoughts from lack-of-money to more-than-enough-money. Think more thoughts of abundance than of lack.

Every decision you make with your money is an investment. To have control over your money and become its master, you must develop a wealthy mindset. Our thoughts, feeling, and attitude about money will influence the outcome of our finances. Wealth is a matter of expectation. If we expect to do well in our finances, then we will begin to think and act accordingly. Those that amass wealth create a habitual attitude and expectation of wealth.

Whatever personal definition you have for wealth, it is essential to understand that wealth is not an accident. It is absolutely predictable and can be earned by anyone. The truth is wealth is no respecter of persons. **Wealth begins on the inside of you; it is a state of mind, just as poverty is a state of mind**. Wealth is not due to luck or circumstances or environment. You have the power to create wealth for yourself. This power was given to you.

If you have not used your power up to this point, then you have no one to blame but yourself. Take responsibility for your life. Your mindset created the life you currently live, and if it is not the life you want, then you and you alone have the power to change it. You need to change your life philosophy if the one you have now is not working for you. Most people's main concern is, "Can I pay my bills?" Life is so much bigger than bills. If you want to change your position in life, you will have to expand your perspective.

> "A mind, like a home, is furnished by its owner, so if one's life is cold and bare, he can blame no one but himself."
> Louis L'Amour

It does not matter where you are spiritually, physically, relationally, or financially today, there is hope. Have confidence in your ability to create the life you truly seek. Being confident is entirely a matter of mind. Without confidence in your own uniqueness, in your GOD-given abilities, you cannot succeed at living a prosperous life. But with self-confidence you can succeed at whatever you choose. So why do we have a large amount of people who are not living a prosperous life if all it takes is believing in themselves? It is because a large percentage of people make themselves unhappy by feeling they are not good enough.

It may be a fact that you are not tall, or able to wear designer clothes or drive a sports car, but you can still become confident. It is attitude that counts. This is not theory.

When I first met my wife, I was only making $6.15 an hour and did not have a college degree. She had a Masters degree and a salary-paying job. When we were dating, my wife never knew how much income I earned. My attitude was that of a multi-millionaire. When she found out I did not have a college education she was in shock, but she could not resist this stud. It was the confidence in myself and my ability to provide that won her over. I knew I was wealthy; it was my mindset, not what I had in my bank account. Honestly, I did not even have a bank account when we were dating. You could not tell me I was not wealthy, I knew it would become my reality in a matter of time.

Now years later, I graduated from college Summa Cum Laude and have multiple streams of income. I did not let anything stand in the way of my progress. You become what you earnestly desire and act upon.

> **"Nobody but YOURSELF can keep you down. You can't expect other people to believe in you, if YOU don't believe in your God given capabilities." Hasheem Francis**

Desire is a force that sets things in motion to bring about its own fulfillment. Thus, to begin fulfilling your desires, you must first do something constructive. There is nothing half-hearted about true desire, it is intense and powerful. If properly developed and expressed, a strong desire can produce great wealth in your life. Only those who become wealth-conscious ever accumulate wealth.

Wealth consciousness means that the mind has become so thoroughly saturated with the desire for wealth, that one can see oneself already in possession of it. **Wealth is about creating: a life of great health,**

loving relationships, doing what you love, and also having money to provide for your needs and help others.

Deuteronomy 8:18 states: **"But thou shalt remember the LORD thy God: for it is he that giveth thee power to get wealth, that he may establish his covenant which he sware unto thy fathers, as it is this day."** God would not give you the power to get wealth if He did not intend for you to use that power and become wealthy! The decision to live in prosperity or poverty is yours. God did His part, now you must do yours by making a life-changing decision today to accept your God-given rights to live abundantly and reject the destructive laws of poverty.

If you have a positive mental attitude towards wealth and you have vigorous faith, you are going to demonstrate wealth in your life. Your attitude is a composite of your thoughts, feelings and actions. The only way you can improve the results you are getting in life, is to take full responsibility for your attitude. Only then will you be able to improve your results. Continue to strive intelligently and persistently to realize your vision. This is the law of prosperity, if you obey the law you will get the results. The law does not discriminate. Prosperity is not an accident and neither is poverty. It is time to reflect on where you are presently and where you want to be in regards to your life.

I would like for you to take a few moments and write in great detail
your answer to the following question: What do you really want out
of life?

_____

_____

_____

_____

_____

_____

_____

_____

_____

_____

_____

_____

_____

_____

_____

_____

_____

_____

_____

_____

What are your personal strengths? Write the qualities you like best about yourself.

_____

_____

_____

_____

_____

_____

_____

_____

_____

_____

_____

_____

_____

_____

_____

_____

_____

_____

_____

_____

_____

_____

What areas of your life need development?

_____

_____

_____

_____

_____

_____

_____

_____

_____

_____

_____

_____

_____

_____

_____

_____

_____

_____

_____

_____

_____

Who would you like to become? Strive to visualize who you want to be in regards to living a life based on your passion.

_____

_____

_____

_____

_____

_____

_____

_____

_____

_____

_____

_____

_____

_____

_____

_____

_____

_____

_____

_____

_____

_____

_____

_____

How do you define wealth, prosperity, and riches?

_____

_____

_____

_____

_____

_____

_____

_____

_____

_____

_____

_____

_____

_____

_____

_____

_____

_____

_____

_____

_____

_____

_____

Are you motivated to achieve what you really want in life?

_____

_____

_____

_____

_____

_____

_____

_____

_____

_____

_____

_____

_____

_____

_____

_____

_____

_____

_____

_____

_____

_____

_____

_____

STOP: Did you complete the exercises? Are you just reading to say you know or are you working for full understanding? I desire the best for you, so if you have not done the exercise and you refuse to participate, put this book down, it is not for the fainthearted. I want results in your life, so please complete all exercises. **Remember, this is your personal journey**. Transformation is never effortless; nothing changes unless YOU do. If you completed the exercises, I applaud your commitment. The reason you must complete the exercises listed is because every time you write your vision or goals you begin to program your desires deeper into your subconscious mind, which can either work for you or against you.

To prosper means you have become prosperous in your mindset. What a person is, not what they have, is the measure of real prosperity. Having an abundant or scarcity mentality affects all areas of your life, not just your bank account. We need a new perspective in redefining what true prosperity and success are, which is the result of having developed a prosperity consciousness, realizing that we all have the necessary tools we need to create our prosperity.

It does not matter what you have achieved or how much cash flow you have coming in, if you live with an attitude of scarcity and limitation, or if you expect for someone or something to fulfill you, you are not going to be satisfied.

When you have a prosperity consciousness, you will have peace of mind, an abundance of wealth, health, and wonderful, loving relationships in life.

You are in charge of your own destiny. All that you need or want is here for the asking. Believe it, and accept it. God's will is to do some powerful and amazing things in your life, and He is ready when you are. Are you tired of living an ordinary life? Wealth is a choice, not a chance. When you really seek to live a life of wealth and abundance, you will.

You become mentally rich when you think rich thoughts. You become emotionally rich when you have rich feelings towards yourself and others. You become spiritually rich when you discover the true riches of the Kingdom within. If you could see a picture of the mental processes of whatever is held in the mind, attracting the things and circumstances that correspond to your thoughts, if you could see the heartaches, the failures, bad health, bad business deals, the debt starting towards you because you have attracted these things in your thoughts, then you would stop worrying and complaining about the things you do not want and start focusing on the things you do want, attracting more abundance instead of lack, success instead of failure.

There is a shocking truth about wealth: wealth adores a person who has a healthy attitude towards it. Your thoughts have made you what you are, and they will make you whatever you become from this day forward. Once you realize this, you will come to a full understanding that people, places, conditions, and events cannot keep wealth from coming to you. This is the power of prosperous thinking.

> "Never say that you can't do something, or that something seems impossible. We are limited only by what we allow ourselves to be limited by: our own mind." Hasheem Francis

When you are prosperous it has a huge impact on your life. It gives you options. It gives you the ability to provide some memorable experiences with your family. It also affects the quality of your relationships, what you eat, the people you can help, what you drive, and where you vacation, and this earth has some beautiful places you will love to visit and experience.

We all have the right to be prosperous. Meditate on those powerful words for a minute and let them become a part of you. **Do you believe you were born to be prosperous and deserve to have more than enough?**

Nevertheless, many people have negative feelings about what it means to prosper. Some even become uncomfortable inside when they get close to personal success and become self destructive. Part of the answer seems to be in how they have defined prosperity and how they may have been programmed with negative thoughts toward it. This programming may have come from their family, the environment they grew up in, or their own limiting beliefs. Getting rid of all the old destructive and erroneous beliefs and developing a true prosperity consciousness requires a total transformation from the inside. You must let go of any old negative concepts of yourself as being inadequate, unsure, unworthy, or any belief that will stand in the way of you creating the life you want.

> "Each of us has a right to life. This means the right to have the free and unrestricted use of all things that may be necessary to our fullest mental, spiritual, and physical unfolding—in other words, our right to be rich." Wallace D. Wattles

You have the ability to be prosperous, but prosperity comes once you first choose to prosper. It is a decision. Through proper planning and consistent action, you can develop a prosperity consciousness that will lead you to wealth as well as increased abundance in all phases of your life. It is wonderful when you come to the full understanding that you have the power to create a life of your choice and you are able to get what you really want and not just what is handed to you. **The power is yours. To increase our prosperity, we must first recognize and appreciate what we have, and we have plenty.**

Wealth alone will never make you happy, but neither will poverty. Rich people have problems and poor people have problems and some of those problems are the same. For example, some rich people take drugs, some poor people takes drugs; some rich people get divorces and poor people get divorces. Happiness has absolutely nothing to do with the presence or absence of material things, but unhappiness can come from a lack of certain material necessities, such as food, clothing, and housing. Happiness has to do primarily with the inner being. If you are not happy on the inside, neither wealth nor poverty will make you happy. You see, neither money nor the lack of it will change your inner being. Abraham Lincoln once stated, **"Most folks are as happy as they make up their minds to be."**

Imagine living your life with the sensation of being fully satisfied, and yet being open to the world. When we understand and apply the principles of prosperity, we know we can handle any turn of events that might take place. We have what it takes to live freely without worry and fear. There is no one thing that needs to happen, no obstacles to get by to start feeling prosperous. We do not need to wait until we have enough of anything in order to be happy. If it is true that we attract only what we are, then let us be all that we can be now.

Let us think for a moment. Say there are two doors in front of you. The first door, once opened, leads to a life of abundance, wealth, prosperity, joy, peace and happiness. The second door, once opened, leads to a life filled with desperation, pain, lack, fear, and a constant state of wanting. You hold the key that can open either door; you choose which door you will open. **It is your choice.**

> **"Every day I have to get up and go put the work in. No matter how many setbacks I experience or how slow the progress, I know I'm still way ahead of where I started." Hasheem Francis**

You must make the decision to live with a mentality of wealth and you will experience lasting freedom. Keep reminding yourself that you have all the power within you that is greater than any current condition or circumstance you may be facing. **Now let us continue our journey!**

CHAPTER I

I AM WHAT I THINK I AM

CHAPTER I
I AM WHAT I THINK I AM

> "Cause and effect is as absolute and undeviating in the hidden realm of thought, as in the world of visible and material things. Mind is the master weaver, both of the interior garment of character and the outer garment of circumstances." James Allen

We are born with the power to create through our thoughts. Our lives are designed by our thoughts, everything originates in our thinking. Each of us is a living magnet. Our thoughts are energy, and we attract into our lives the people and circumstances that harmonize with our most dominant thoughts. Our thought energy has the power to create from the world of ideas to the world of reality.

Our life at this present moment is the representation of our thought patterns. Our greatest and most priceless possession is our mind. Mind is creative, and if we desire to attract different people, circumstances, events, we have to change what is going on in our minds and thought patterns.

Wealth begins in the mind; God has given us a powerful and creative tool. We receive this power to create from our ability to use our imagination. Everything that has been created by someone was first an imaginative idea. We are surrounded by creative ideas that have manifested into the physical reality.

Our mind is a spiritual estate. The results we receive in life and in our businesses are shaped by our dominant thoughts, our beliefs, and our attitude. It is amazing how many people allow their limited thinking to determine how much they accomplish or strive for in life.

> "Thought is the only power that can produce tangible riches from the formless substance." Wallace D. Wattles

We can change our circumstances by changing the way we think, feel, what we believe, what we say to ourselves, and the actions we take. However, the secret of prosperity is that it begins within your own thoughts and feeling. There is a powerful magnet within you that attracts to you what you are.

I have noticed that people who may have had some sort of destructive relationship in their life continue to attract those same types of people. Hurt people attract hurt people, abundance attracts abundance and lack attracts lack. This was a wake-up call for me once I realized I was focusing more on what I did not want and not on what I desired. I used to literally spend hours of the day focusing on how I was going to pay my bills. I gave those bills a lot of power, putting so much worry into not having enough to pay them.

I was acting like the bill collectors were the boogie monster coming to eat me. Thinking about them continually created a feeling of fear, and then I began to talk in fear and act in fear. My thoughts became energy that manifested itself into a late bill. We attract everything that happens in our life.

> "When you stand before a mirror, YOU are looking into the eyes of your best friend and your worst enemy. Who YOU invest the most time in, will determine the outcome of your life." Hasheem Francis

Once we focus our thoughts on things we want, and feel as though they are so, we give those desires energy to manifest themselves in our lives.

It is imperative that we think in keeping with our divine inheritance, which is prosperity. King David stated one of the most powerful declarations there is: "The Lord is my shepherd, I shall not want."

We cannot attract or develop a prosperity mentality by a scarcity-stricken attitude that drives away what we seek. We must think prosperity before we can come to it. **Whatever your mind is taught to expect, it will build, produce, and bring forth for you.**

A scarcity mentality is the opposite of the prosperity mentality. People that function under a scarcity mentality believe that there is never enough in life: never enough love, enough money, or enough opportunities. When you function under this mentality of never enough, you restrict your creative ability to produce, and you begin to act in haste because you believe someone else is going to get what you desire. Our expectations affect our results.

What are your expectations about life? Do you feel you have a
purpose in life? Describe what you want to contribute to the world.

_____

_____

_____

_____

_____

_____

_____

_____

_____

_____

_____

_____

_____

_____

_____

_____

_____

_____

_____

_____

The reason why most people are unhappy is that they are living under the expectation and programming of others. Most of our programming has been influenced by negative thoughts—not only our own thoughts, but all of those around us. Our parents, our friends, even the television can program you with the wrong expectations of life. It is a cycle that must be broken. The Apostle Paul wrote in Romans 12:2: **"And be not conformed to this world: but be ye transformed by the renewing of your mind, that ye may prove what is that good, and acceptable, and perfect, will of God."**

It is important that you set your own expectation in everything you do in life. Always expect the best from yourself, always expect to continue to get better. You are doing that now, and that is why you are reading this book. **Whatever we expect with conviction becomes our own self-fulfilling prophecy**. Through their thoughts, most people are often attracting things to themselves that they do not consciously desire. Your thoughts are creative not because you wish, hope, pray, or long for it to be so. They are creative because there is a creative law operating upon them. **You are where and what you are because of the dominant thoughts in your mind**.

> **"As a man thinketh in his heart, so is he." King Solomon**

Think big because you are big. Think generously because you are made to express generosity. There are no limits except the limits you place on your own imagination. Stop chasing after lack; instead come to the full understanding that wealth was custom made just for you. It is certain that you cannot believe in wealth, prosperity, and abundance if you identify yourself as an individual of lack. Forget the lack and think only of wealth in all areas of your life.

You have absolute control over one thing, and that is your thoughts. You cannot control the weather, your kids, spouse, or anything for that matter outside of your own beliefs, thoughts, attitudes, and actions. **You are the key that will unlock the door to your desires**, so concentrate on what you do have control over—your thoughts. And that can be the most powerful control of all. Prosperity belongs to you, and it will only come to you if you affirm its presence in your thoughts.

Your mind must create the good you want, for then and only then will you experience the good you have created. **You can produce definite results only when your mind has been given definite desires**. Your only limitation is in your mind. If there is failure and lack in your life, it is because you first imagined it in your mind.

"Those who earn the most, are willing to work. Do not complain about someone else's results, if YOU are not willing to put the work in. Don't except your own excuses" Hasheem Francis

We have the power to change, to be what we want to be, to have what we want to have. That power is thought. When our thoughts are repeated often enough, they form a pattern. These thought patterns actually program our minds. Whatever we are programming our minds to create, it creates. Successful people think about what they want, and how to get it, most of the time. When you think and talk about what you want, and how to get it, you feel happier and in greater control of your life.

We all aspire to have the best and to live a full and complete life. God's plan of redemption includes your redemption from self-imposed limitations. Some people have a hard time accepting that life is not all about struggling and that it is completely fine to live a life of abundance. Many would even argue that being poor is noble, that is their opinion. I do not believe that nor have the desire to understand that type of thinking.

We all have been given all the necessary tools and power to create the life we seek. Some people need to enlarge their vision of what they want to do in their lives and come to a full understanding of wealth. As long as your mind is working, you can do extraordinary things.

Your thoughts and your willingness to take action are the only attributes that stand in your way of attaining what you want in life. You can have what you think you deserve, and what you believe you can have. If you are convinced you should not have or are unworthy of getting what you want, you will unconsciously create an environment that will prevent you from becoming successful. Unsuccessful people think and talk about things they do not want. They think and talk about their problems and pains, and the people they do not like. Sometimes, their whole lives revolve around their complaints and criticisms, and the more they think and complain about what they do not want, the unhappier they become. My mentor shared an insight with me a couple years ago: **"Small people talk about people, average people talk about events, and wealthy people talk about ideas."**

Learn to think abundantly. Think of the vastness of everything; like the limitless of space, or the grains of sand on the seashore which cannot be counted. Think how abundant, how lavish, how rich nature is. Develop a habit of seeing abundance in everything, to multiply the good you already possess. Be conscious of the law of abundance. As you develop a consciousness of prosperity, you will experience improvement in life.

"Make every thought, every fact, that comes into your mind pay you a profit. Make it work and produce for you. Think of things not as they are but as they might be. Don't merely dream, but create." Robert Collier

It is important that you maintain a strict censorship over your thinking. Just as a gardener watches over their garden to protect it from weeds and anything that can destroy the beauty of the garden, so you must refuse entrance to any thoughts you do not wish to see manifested in your life. What you accept completely in your mind, you will get in experience, regardless of conditions, or circumstances. So what is keeping you from believing in yourself and achieving your goals? Your self-limiting thoughts and you can conquer those.

Guard your mind at all cost; it is the garden of your soul. It is your garden where your hopes, dreams, and desires are blossoming into fulfillment. If you allow the weeds of fear, doubt, and hatred, to grow in the garden of your mind, it will choke out the beauty of hope until despair alone remains. The way to eliminate the self doubt that holds many prisoners is by: filling your mind with faith in the Creator who created you in His image and this will give you a powerful, realistic faith in yourself. Reprogram your mind to be confident instead of self critical. **Make positive expectations the default of your thinking. Turn your mind into a prosperous thinking, power producing machine.** Plant in the garden of your mind seeds of love, joy, wealth, abundance, peace, gratitude, and happiness.

Exercise: Turn off the television and take the battery out the phone (I know taking the battery out is a little extreme, but peace and quiet comes at a cost). Set aside at least 20 minutes a day to clear your mind. Find a quiet place away from all the distractions and get comfortable. Close your eyes, and let your thoughts flow freely. This can be quite difficult when you start this exercise, but practice. Practice and stick with it, until you learn how to quiet your mind from outside distractions. You will feel refreshed afterwards. You may find this very relaxing.

It is a known fact that thoughts often repeated form patterns in the mind which automatically reproduce themselves. Form in your mind a mental picture of yourself succeeding and living a prosperous life. Never permit it to fade. Disregard all thoughts of doubt and failure, hold to your mental image of success.

The mind always tries to complete what it pictures, so always picture a prosperous life, no matter how difficult your current circumstances may be. Whenever a negative thought about your ability to create a prosperous life comes to mind, deliberately voice a positive thought to cancel it out. I have developed the habit of when a negative thought comes to my mind, I always voice out loud: "I rebuke that." I am basically telling my mind I do not agree with that thought, I must think of something better.

We will always draw to ourselves what we focus on. If we are to attract and have what we desire in life, we must first think it forth. We will always manifest what we think. In order to have success, we must first conceive it in our own thought. Never let doubt creep in for even a minute. Always be positive about yourself and your desires. **Keep watch over the inner working of your thoughts, and the law of prosperity will do the rest.**

> **"Life will pay YOU exactly what you think you're worth. Nothing more. If you want to EARN more, value yourself and become more." Deborah Francis**

You must surround yourself with a positive atmosphere and keep all negative thoughts that suggest discord, disaster, and failure out of your mind. Hold only those thoughts, words, and pictures which builds you up and pushes you towards your vision. Center your attention on what you want and you will automatically draw it to you. You will only get what you accept in life, and if you are not satisfied with your current result, start thinking about your life the way you want it to be.

When you expect great things in your life, you will receive them.
Expect success, love, joy, prosperity, great relationships, health, and
good to come to you. By the law of concentration, whatever you dwell
upon grows and increases in your life. So, think about what you want
and keep your mind off what you do not want. Think about what you
desire in life.

> "Finally, brethren, whatsoever things are true, whatsoever
> things are honest, whatsoever things are just, whatsoever
> things are pure, whatsoever things are lovely, whatsoever
> things are of good report; if there be any virtue, and if there be
> any praise, think on these things." Philippians 4:8

Expect lavish abundance in your life every day in every way and you
will soon change the character of your entire mind. Every time we
focus our thoughts on something, we are producing and creating
something, so why not create wealth? Wealth is the result of deliberate
thoughts and actions. There is no hit or miss with prosperous living.
**To become the master of your destiny, you must learn to control
the nature of your dominant, habitual thoughts**.

Key points:
- Be the gardener of your mind. Watch what is poured into it.
- What you desire is already available to you.
- Be conscious of the abundance within you.
- You are a creator, create what you desire.
- You always get what you focus on.

Built To Prosper "Thought" Quotes

"These thoughts did not come in any verbal formulation. I rarely think in words at all. A thought comes, and I may try to express it in words afterward."
Albert Einstein

"Always aim at complete harmony of thought in word and deed. Always aim at purifying your thoughts and everything will be well."
Mahatma Gandhi

"Thought is the blossom; language the bud; action the fruit behind it."
Ralph Waldo Emerson

"You are today where your thoughts have brought you; you will be tomorrow where your thoughts take you."
James Allen

"All my life I have tried to pluck a thistle and plant a flower wherever the flower would grow in thought and mind."
Abraham Lincoln

"Being self-disciplined begins with the mastery of your thoughts. If you don't control what you think, you can't control what you do. Simply, self-discipline enables you to think first and act afterward."
Napoleon Hill

"The environment you fashion out of your thoughts, your beliefs, your ideals, your philosophy is the only climate you will ever live in. The key is in not spending time, but in investing it."
Stephen R. Covey

CHAPTER II

GUARD YOUR MOUTH

CHAPTER II
GUARD YOUR MOUTH

"If someone were to pay you ten cents for every kind word you ever spoke and collect from you five cents for every unkind word, would YOU be rich or poor?"

Words are the most powerful thing in the universe. Words are energy, and energy is creative. Spoken words program your spirit either for success or defeat, abundance or lack, hope or despair. Have you heard someone continually say he wants to be financially free and then in the next sentence confess he is broke? I once heard someone say, "What you argue for, you keep." The level of your success begins in your mind and in your mouth. Many people are unaware that they literally speak things into existence. Their mouth is one of the causes of their circumstances.

Every time you say, "I am broke," "I am stupid," or "I am poor," you are giving power to everything that you are not. Your words are powerful, so speak specific words of wealth for yourself. Speak words of life and not of death. In what direction are your words leading you: to the path of abundance, or down the path of scarcity?

"If the word has the potency to revive and make us free, it has also the power to blind, imprison, and destroy." Ralph Ellison

You need to speak what you desire. You should never underestimate the power of the spoken word. You can actually transform your life by the words you speak.

I remember when I was working for one of the largest Fortune 500 companies, I was having lunch with one of the top executives and asked him, "What does a company look for in a leader when he or she is being considered for one of the top positions in the company?" He said, "We can tell a lot about a person by the words they use." **If you listen closely to what someone is truly saying, he will reveal his true character**. Those words of wisdom stayed with me. It literally saved me from partnering with some people who lacked integrity in business.

We are the authors of our life and the words we speak are the story everyone sees, reads, and hear. Our thoughts, words, and feelings become flesh and live with us; they become our environment and surround us. In order to create the life you truly want you must speak words of faith, power, and victory.

Make it a practice to replace those negative words in your personal vocabulary with positive words. Instead of doubtful words, plant words of hope, instead of defeating words, plant words of victory, instead of fearful words, plant words of encouragement, instead of hateful and bitter words, plant and use words of love. If you continue this practice and apply it consistently and persistently every day, you will create a life of true fulfillment. All of the power is in your tongue, so begin speaking the good you seek in your life; learn to speak what your heart desires.

> **"Your own words are the bricks and mortar of the dreams you want to realize. Your words are the greatest power you have. The words you choose and their use establish the life you experience." Sonia Choquette**

Many people fail at achieving their goals in life because of their words. They put themselves down before they even set out. Sit down with a family member or friend and have them share with you their dreams, aspirations, or a goal they always wanted to achieve and ask them why they never took action to accomplish it. They may say something like, "It was just a dream, I do not think I could really achieve it."

The spoken word has a tremendous impact on both your external and internal reality. **Words are powerful. The words you speak are seeds that produce fruit after their kind**. Whatever you say eventually comes back to you like a boomerang. Just as sure as you plant them, you can be equally sure a harvest will follow.

You can have what you say when you learn to release faith from the heart in your words. I used to say the word "worry" when I was in college. Every time a professor would make us aware that we were having an exam so we could take time to study, my reply was, "I'm not worried about it." But when exam time came around I found myself worrying.

I did not notice what was causing most of my worries until I got married. My wife Deborah would ask me to do things like pack my clothes the night before a business trip, or get the kids' clothes ready for school, or take the car in for an oil change. I would reply, "I'm not worried about it," then when the time came, I found myself rushing to pack, or I was not able to find the proper clothes for the kids or the engine light was on in my car.

My wife took notice and encouraged me to change what I was saying. She became my accountability partner, and when I tell you she held me accountable, with consequences. As soon as she thought I was going to say the word "worry" she gave me my warning. This is a PG book, so I cannot share my punishment. I will just say I removed that word from my vocabulary immediately. That negative word was keeping me from experiencing peace in my life. I now speak words of faith and victory over my life. **Successful, happy people think and talk about what they want most of the time.**

> "Never change things by fighting the existing reality, to change something build a new model that makes the old model obsolete." Bob Proctor

Every day we must decide to make positive declarations over our lives. Speak words that uplift you, that ignite a fire in you to propel you towards success. You have one life; this is the only chance you have, and there is no retake. God created you to do great things, so declare words of greatness. Your thoughts and words have power to produce the life you give it. **Your words contain energy that brings the fruit of those words back to you.**

Do the words you use bring you: Abundance or lack, faith or fear, hope or despair?

_____

_____

_____

_____

_____

_____

_____

_____

You were made to achieve the unthinkable. Success and wealth desires you more than you know. The only person that can stop wealth from showing up is you. Your words reveal a great deal about your character. The words you use are the reflection of how you see yourself and life.

Complainers

Do you know someone—a family member, friend, or co-worker—who always complains? It does not matter what the subject or the season, all they do is complain. They always finds something wrong. It could be a beautiful day and they would be complaining about it being too hot. People who complain all of the time are really unhappy people. They are frustrated with the results of their lives, and as a result, they become critical of everyone and everything around them. They only see life through their foggy, gloomy glasses, which obscure their view on situations and people. Success never comes easy for the complainers, and if they do succeed they will complain about all the hard work it took.

> "The loudest and most influential voice you hear is your own inner voice, your self critic. It can work for you or against you, depending on the messages you allow." Keith Harrell

There are two roads, one that leads to prosperity and one that leads to scarcity, and they travel in opposite directions. If you desire prosperity, you must with all your heart, mind, and soul refuse to think or speak of any circumstances that lead toward scarcity.

If you study any successful person's life, you will observe that they had control over what went into their mind and the words that come out of their mouth. People who achieve a great deal of success live and honor their words. I remember when I was young and we used to say, "My word is bond." That meant we stood behind the words that came out of our mouth 100%. There were no money back guarantees; all you had was your word. **You are a creative spiritual being: think and speak accordingly. Begin now to speak blessings over everything and everyone who is and comes into your life**. It is just as easy to speak good as it is to condemn and complain. Your words reveal what is in your heart. When you condemn and complain, you intensify unpleasant conditions in your life. Start speaking words of love, victory, peace, and success in your home, relationships and business. I came to the understanding that before I can expect anyone to say anything positive and encouraging to me, I must first talk to myself in such a manner.

I like to refer to the wisdom of "the richest man who ever lived," King Solomon. I believe he is a great man to learn from. In the Book of Proverbs, King Solomon has much to say about thevalue of well-chosen words.

King Solomon's Wisdom from the Book of Proverbs

"A gentle answer turns away wrath, but a harsh word stirs up anger." Proverbs. 15:1

"Pleasant words are as an honeycomb, Sweet to the soul and healing to the bones." Proverbs 16:24

"Anxiety in the heart of a man weighs it down, But a good word makes it glad." Proverbs 12:25

"For my mouth shall speak truth; and wickedness is an abomination to my lips." Proverbs 6:7

"All the words of my mouth are in righteousness; there is nothing froward or perverse in them." Proverbs 6:8

"Thou art snared with the words of thy mouth, thou art taken with the words of thy mouth." Proverbs 6:2

"The mouth of a righteous man is a well of life: but violence covereth the mouth of the wicked." Proverbs 10:11

"Wise men lay up knowledge: but the mouth of the foolish is near destruction." Proverbs 10:14

"A man hath joy by the answer of his mouth: and a word spoke in due season, how good is it!" Proverbs 10:23

"In the multitude of words there wanteth not sin: but he that refraineth his lips is wise." Proverbs 10:19

"The tongue of the just is as choice silver: the heart of the wicked is little worth." Proverbs 10:20

King Solomon's Wisdom from the Book of Proverbs

"The lips of the righteous feed many: but fools die for want of wisdom." Proverbs 10:21

"The mouth of the just bringeth forth wisdom: but the froward tongue shall be cut out." Proverbs 10:31

"The lips of the righteous know what is acceptable: but the mouth of the wicked speaketh frowardness." Proverbs 10:32

"A man shall be satisfied with good by the fruit of his mouth: and the recompence of a man's hands shall be rendered unto him." Proverbs 12:14

"There is that speaketh like the piercings of a sword: but the tongue of the wise is health." Proverbs 12:18

"A man shall eat good by the fruit of his mouth: but the soul of the transgressors shall eat violence." Proverbs 13:2

"He that keepeth his mouth keepeth his life: but he that openeth wide his lips shall have destruction." Proverbs 13:3

"Go from the presence of a foolish man, when thou perceivest not in him the lips of knowledge." Proverbs 14:7

"The tongue of the wise useth knowledge aright: but the mouth of fools poureth out foolishness." Proverbs 15:2

"A wholesome tongue is a tree of life: but perverseness therein is a breach in the spirit." Proverbs 15:4

<u>King Solomon's Wisdom from the Book of Proverbs</u>

"The preparations of the heart in man, and the answer of the tongue, is from the LORD." Proverbs 16:1

"The heart of the wise teacheth his mouth, and addeth learning to his lips." Proverbs 16:23

"The words of a man's mouth are as deep waters, and the wellspring of wisdom as a flowing brook." Proverbs 18:4

"A fool's lips enter into contention, and his mouth calleth for strokes." Proverbs 18:6

"A fool's mouth is his destruction, and his lips are the snare of his soul." Proverbs 18:7

"The words of a talebearer are as wounds, and they go down into the innermost parts of the belly." Proverbs 18:8

"A man's belly shall be satisfied with the fruit of his mouth; and with the increase of his lips shall he be filled." Proverbs 18:20

"Death and life are in the power of the tongue: and they that love it shall eat the fruit thereof." Proverbs 18:21

"Whoso keepeth his mouth and his tongue keepeth his soul from troubles." Proverbs 21:23

"Speak not in the ears of a fool: for he will despise the wisdom of thy words." Proverbs 23:9

The Power of Affirmations

An affirmation is a positive thought spoken aloud and held with the conviction to produce a desired result. As you speak affirmatively, you will develop a new image on the inside, and things will begin to change in your favor. Nothing is more powerful and creative than affirmative words. Your words have a positive life force in them when used properly. What we need are affirmations that will empower us, encourage us, and change us for the better, enabling us to go further and reach higher than we ever dreamed possible.

Exercise: Over the next 21 days, your goal is to develop the habit of speaking positive affirmations to yourself. Each day for the next 21 days, write your positive affirmation and declare it out loud at least three times during the day and night with intense feelings. Continue this until it becomes a part of you, form the habit. The more you hear them, the more you believe they will come to pass. Unless you are fully committed to changing your life, do not start the process. If you do not intend on completing the exercise, do not start, if you do start, go all the way. All out commitment. Make your mind up and do it! **Example:**

I AM ABUNDANCE, I AM A CHEERFUL GIVER.

1. I AM _____
2. I AM _____
3. I AM _____
4. I AM _____
5. I AM _____
6. I AM _____
7. I AM _____
8. I AM _____
9. I AM _____
10. I AM _____
11. I AM _____
12. I AM _____
13. I AM _____
14. I AM _____
15. I AM _____
16. I AM _____
17. I AM _____
18. I AM _____
19. I AM _____
20. I AM _____
21. I AM _____

Commit to it! As you say these faith filled words, your faith will be strengthened. The more you hear them, the more you will believe that they will surely come to pass. After you have written the affirmation, repeat it over and over with feeling, with confidence, with belief and enthusiasm, so these powerful words can be programmed into your subconscious mind. These affirmative words will sink from your conscious mind into your subconscious mind and in time change the way you think. It is your subconscious mind that is the storehouse of your deep-rooted beliefs. To change your circumstances and attract what you desire, you must learn to reprogram your subconscious mind. This process will help condition your mind for success. What is important to understand is that your subconscious mind cannot distinguish between fact and fiction. It accepts the images you construct while writing and reviewing your affirmation.

If you are willing to invest the time and effort required to develop a new habit of thought, you can become all that you desire. The power of speaking faith into your life delivers your heart's desires to you. It is not enough to think and act on your heart's desires, it is important that you declare it aloud. Say it both to yourself and to anyone who will support and encourage you to succeed. You need to keep speaking faith into your life until the results manifest in your life.

Affirming words of faith into your life truly delivers better results. You may have had setbacks, but it is time for you to start speaking change into your circumstances. As you think and act towards a better, prosperous life, add the affirmation aspect to the process. No matter how short or long the journey is, you will surely have what you say.

Whatever the conscious mind believes and accepts, the subconscious mind immediately goes to work to bring into our physical reality. We have to keep talking to ourselves as though we already have what we want. Only thoughts with intense feelings bring results. Most people are defeated because they do not commit to personal growth and they believe and confess the wrong things. The defeated speak the words of the enemy, and those words hold them in bondage. Negative statements tend to destroy any good we look to start.

So, begin declaring how prosperous and loved you are, how you are wealthy, healthy, victorious, abundantly supplied, joyful, peaceful, and happy. You deserve better results in your life, so engage in the power of affirming words of faith and you will enjoy a most successful life. Your confessions will change your life. Your words give your life focus and attention.

Key points:

- Speak words of truth, faith and victory.
- You can have what you say.
- Your tongue holds the power of life and death.
- You are the author of your life and your words create the story.
- Speak positive declarations daily.

Built To Prosper "Power of Words" Quotes:

"Words do two major things: They provide food for the mind and create light for understanding and awareness."
Jim Rohn

"If someone were to pay you ten cents for every kind word you ever spoke and collect from you five cents for every unkind word, would you be rich or poor?"
Unknown

"Think twice before you speak, because your words and influence will plant the seed of either success or failure in the mind of another."
Napoleon Hill

"Kind words are short and easy to speak, but their echoes are truly endless."
Mother Teresa

"We will have to give an account on the day of judgment for every careless word spoken."
Mathew 12:36

"Words are the keys to the heart."
Chinese proverb

"Perhaps you will forget tomorrow the kind words you say today, but the recipient may cherish them for a lifetime."
Dale Carnegie

CHAPTER III

MY ATTITUDE IS EITHER MY FRIEND OR FOE

CHAPTER III
MY ATTITUDE IS EITHER MY FRIEND OR FOE

> "Everything can be taken from a man but...the last of the human freedoms—to choose one's attitude in any given set of circumstances, to choose one's own way." Victor Frankl

Your attitude affects all areas of your life. Our attitude comes from our expectations about life. If we expect things to be wonderful, we will have a positive attitude. If we expect things to turn out for the worst, things have a tendency to turn out that way. Your attitude is the most visible manifestation of you as a person. A positive mental attitude is the driving force that will assist you as you set out to achieve all that you want in life. It takes discipline to consistently have a positive attitude, especially when you are dealing with difficult people or situations.

You will be challenged, but the challenges come to strengthen your attitude. When you can smile in the face of opposition and keep a positive attitude no matter what the circumstances are around you, then you have fully developed an attitude that will propel you towards success. I know you may be thinking to yourself, "Yeah right, Mr. Sunny man, do you smile every time you are faced with a difficult situation?" And my answer is, "Not all the time; it is a work in progress. I am human just like you." There are times when I do not feel like being positive; I call those days oh-woe-is-me days. But I learned, and it took time and discipline to not allow myself to get stuck with a negative attitude. I also have an accountability partner who holds me accountable when I am in that negative state. My accountability partner is quick to call me on it. I may not want to hear what she has to say, but I know she has my best interest at heart.

The most successful people view their attitude as a valuable asset that deserves protection and attention. Most often people with a negative attitude do not get far in life. Their attitude about life holds them back and they become what you would call a light dimmer. As soon as they walk in the room the lights dim; they drain all the positive energy in the room with their attitude. Successful people stay clear of people with negative attitudes. Have you ever spent time with someone who constantly complains about everything and as soon as you leave him you find yourself complaining? When we share time with others our attitude often sets the tone for how we treat one another.

There is nothing in life as dangerous as a negative attitude. No one who was negative about themselves and their opportunities in life has ever achieved lasting success. You must learn to cast negative, destructive thinking aside and focus on the positive. One of the steps to developing a positive attitude is to become aware of your current attitude. In order to succeed in building a life filled with prosperity you need to approach life with a positive or affirmative attitude.

The quality of your life will depend mostly on your attitude. An optimistic attitude attracts optimistic people. A negative, constantly complaining attitude attracts negative, constantly complaining people. Until you change your thoughts, it will continue to form your attitude, which will be the prevailing way you choose to see the world throughout your life, causing you to strictly limit your life's vision and impose tight boundaries around your beliefs.

Your life is affected by your habit of thinking and attitude of mind. Your attitude is a composite of your thoughts, feelings, and actions. The only way you can improve the results you are getting in life is to take full responsibility for your attitude. Only then will you be able to improve your results. Your thoughts influence all your actions, thus helping to manifest—or attract to you—an environment that corresponds to your thoughts. This is why the quality of your thinking is so instrumental in forming your world view and explains why the most successful people guard and fortify their thoughts, and take the time to think about what they are thinking about. **Your attitude reflects your thoughts**.

Your attitude is either your friend or foe. Attitude is the criterion for success. Developing a positive or negative attitude is a choice. No one can give you a great attitude. It is something you must develop for yourself. (It would be great to borrow a positive attitude on those difficult days.)

If you desire to make your life a masterpiece, then you need to have the right attitude about different areas of your life. Your real change in life comes from within. It is your own attitude that demands your focus. The key to prosperity is to change your thoughts and attitude about yourself and your success. It takes time to design the life you desire. Most people want a quick fix and when something they want does not come immediately, they quit. As Napoleon Hill stated, **"Winners never quit, and quitters never win."**

You will see your desires come to pass if you believe and refuse to give up. Whatever you do, do not let the delays in achieving your goals affect your attitude. A delay is not a denial. How would you feel if you told everyone you were going to be financially free in one year and you do not achieve that goal? **Would you feel like a failure? Or would you continue to go after your goal?**

Fear of failure keeps many from taking necessary risks, but the willingness to take risks and step out on faith is a measure of your prosperity consciousness. **One way to overcome fear is to ask yourself, "What is the worst thing that could happen if I failed at something I really wanted?"** If you can live with the results, then get out there and go for it.

Our highs in life come not from having or surmounting any single challenge, but from the strength we experience when we find the means within us to face a challenge and overcome the barriers to resolution. We get energy when we take risks and act in spite of our fears.

> **"Most people achieved their greatest success one step beyond what looked like their greatest failure." Brian Tracy**

Since your thoughts influence your attitude, it is essential to continually work to improve your quality of thinking. To develop a positive attitude towards wealth, family, health, and prosperity we need to take an assessment of your current attitude.

What are your positive qualities and negative tendencies?

_____

_____

_____

_____

_____

_____

_____

_____

_____

_____

_____

_____

_____

_____

_____

_____

_____

_____

_____

_____

_____

What type of person would your family and friends describe you as?

_____

_____

_____

_____

_____

_____

_____

_____

_____

_____

_____

_____

_____

_____

_____

_____

_____

_____

_____

_____

What is your attitude towards prosperity and those that are prosperous?

_____

_____

_____

_____

_____

_____

_____

_____

_____

_____

_____

_____

_____

_____

_____

_____

_____

_____

_____

_____

_____

_____

_____

Do you believe a person of great wealth achieved his or her success through honesty, integrity, and commitment, or through greed and by taking advantage of others? Why?

_____

_____

_____

_____

_____

_____

_____

_____

_____

_____

_____

_____

_____

_____

_____

_____

_____

_____

When I began to develop a prosperity consciousness, my attitude was that I was going to be kind, loving, generous, and a happy, wealthy man. I did not want to be like the wealthy people displayed on television. When I was growing up, the pictures I recalled of the wealthy was through various television programs we watched in our home on a regular basis such as *Duck Tales* with Scrooge McDuck, who was a miserable individual, Mr. Howell from *Gilligan's Island*, who was snobby, and Mr. George Jefferson from *The Jeffersons*, who was rude.

I did not know many real life millionaires so I could only go on what I saw on TV (the idiot box) and what broke people told me. Once I got to really know wealthy people, I realized they were nothing like what I have seen or heard. They were some of the most kind-hearted people who were doing a great deal of philanthropic work around the country. It is truly amazing how we allow others who do not have full knowledge or wealth to dictate our attitude towards wealth.

Your attitude governs the way you act, the way the action will unfold, and the reward or consequences of your action. You must examine your personal attitude continuously towards wealth because it has a huge impact on your life. **Your attitude is what separates you from the crowd**. It is easy to live and be a part of the crowd: just watch what they watch, talk how they talk, read what they read, do what they do and you will get what they got. To get the results you envision and live abundantly, you must do everything you can to separate yourself from those who will pull you down while you develop your dream.

> **"A dreamer is one who can only find his way by moonlight, and his punishment is that he sees the dawn before the rest of the world." Oscar Wilde**

Your attitude is shaped by many factors: personality, environment, self-image, the positive or negative expressions of others, and your thoughts. No matter what you seek to achieve, your attitude is a vital part of that success. Your attitude about yourself, your potential, your ability, your unique capacity to achieve, will in a large part set the limits on what you do achieve.

Attitude of Gratitude

The best attitude you can possibly aspire to express is one of gratitude and appreciation for the things you value most in life. Being grateful for what you already have in your life attracts more good to you. When you are grateful you open the door for abundance to flow. By focusing your thoughts and attention on the abundance that is already present in your life, you could create a positive attitude that will attract more to be grateful for. Keep in mind that feeling prosperous is fully enjoying what you already have. Right now we all have resources we are not using, resources that can be appreciated now. **A thankful heart is one that has taken the time to count the blessings**. Take a moment and really feel the emotion of gratitude.

> "Many people who order their lives rightly in all other ways are kept in poverty by their lack of gratitude." Wallace D. Wattles

What five things are you grateful for?

_____

_____

_____

_____

_____

Part of your success depends upon your gratitude and recognition that God is your source. God is the one who supplies everything you need. Anything good in your life is a blessing from Him. Living with an attitude of gratitude is without doubt the best way to live life.

I am grateful you have committed to being all that God created you to be!

Attitude of Giving
What is your attitude about giving? Are you a cheerful giver?

_____

_____

_____

_____

_____

_____

_____

As you give, so shall you receive. If you do not sow, you cannot reap. In all of life, receiving depends upon giving. Some people feel they have nothing to give. **Most people think giving is only about money, but there is love, joy, laughter, and encouragement you can give**.

The only way to experience a harvest is to be a sower. If you sow love you will reap love; sow finances and you will reap finances. If you desire more money to meet your needs, be a generous money sower, and in due season you will reap a harvest. When you become a giver, you automatically move yourself into the realm of a receiver. There are no exceptions to this rule. This is the law of sowing and reaping. You will receive everything that you give. **"Give, and it shall be given unto you..." Luke 6:38**

If you begin to understand your God-given right of giving, there will come a day when the prosperity of God will literally overtake you. You will have more than enough to share with others with plenty left over to meet your family's every need and your own. When you are a cheerful giver, God will bless you and give you back many blessings out of His abundance!

> "If you desire to become a more generous person, don't wait for your income to change. Change your heart." John C. Maxwell

Key points:

- Your attitude will determine your level of success.
- A positive or a negative attitude is a choice.
- Read positive books. There are plenty at the library and it is a free membership.
- Make a habit of sharing and giving to others.
- Hold loving thoughts towards yourself and others.
- Limit your time talking to, watching, or listening to negative information (ex. doom and gloom friends, the news, or moody music).

<u>Built To Prosper "Attitude" Quotes:</u>

"There is little difference in people, but that little difference makes a big difference. The little difference is attitude. The big difference is whether it is positive or negative."
W. Clement Stone

"You cannot control what happens to you, but you can control your attitude toward what happens to you, and in that, you will be mastering change rather than allowing it to master you."
Brian Tracy

"Your mental attitude is something you can control outright and you must use self-discipline until you create a positive mental attitude. Your mental attitude attracts to you everything that makes you what you are."
Napoleon Hill

"Weakness of attitude becomes weakness of character."
Albert Einstein

"It is your attitude, not your aptitude, that determines your altitude."
Zig Ziglar

"Ability is what you're capable of doing. Motivation determines what you do. Attitude determines how well you do it."
Lou Holtz

"The last of the human freedoms is to choose one's attitude in any given set of circumstances."
Victor E. Frankl

CHAPTER IV

WHOSE REPORT DO YOU BELIEVE?

CHAPTER IV
WHOSE REPORT DO YOU BELIEVE?

> "Now, you are the sum total of what you believe, good and bad: what you have accepted in mind, what motivating thoughts and acts as a result of your belief. As your beliefs change, your life will change with them, for your life is really based upon faith." Claude M. Bristol

The impossible begins to happen when a positive attitude evolves into belief. The beliefs we have about ourselves and life are responsible for who we ultimately become and what we eventually achieve in life. What you believe to be true is true and nothing else. Belief is the power behind our creative thoughts. Thought alone is not enough to manifest an idea into physical reality. It must be combined with belief. Every aspect of your life, from the state of your health to the state of your relationships and finances, is accurately revealing your thoughts and your beliefs.

Before we can begin to create a vision for what it is we want to do in life, we must first believe we are capable of achieving whatever it is we desire. Without this belief, we would never even attempt to do anything about our dreams. As Otis Redding sang, "We'll be sitting on the dock of the bay, watching the tides roll away...wasting time."

Do you believe you will prosper? Are you an optimist or a pessimist?

The difference between an optimist and pessimist is the optimist mindset says "I will see it when I believe it." The pessimist says "I will believe it when I see it." Optimists seem to have different ways of dealing with the world that set them apart from the average. They keep their minds on what they want, and keep looking for ways to get it.

"Do not limit yourself today. YOU can go as far as your mind lets you. Learning new things never exhaust the mind"
Hasheem Francis

Most negative people do not believe in themselves, so they decide not to make an attempt at changing their lives. Some people believe they are stuck in their ways and there is no hope for them to ever change. They have what you would call "The Al Bundy Syndrome" (as in Al Bundy from the television show "Married with Children"). Bundy was a depressed husband, father, and down-on-his-luck shoe salesman. In every episode of the show, Al believed that no good would come to him, and guess what Al got? Exactly what he expected.

Another reason many may not believe in themselves is they may be holding on to past mistakes. Realize that if you do not let go of past failures, frustrations, or rejection, then you simply are not available to create your future with more productive levels of thinking that lead to more effective actions and results. **We cannot go and relive the past; the focus must be on today and today only**.

If you study the lives of those who have achieved success or have had a huge impact on others' lives, you will see many have made mistakes and had setbacks, but continued to pursue their goals. When they experienced setbacks their mind held the belief of their end result, accomplishing what they set out to do. Today is your day to create your success. Your today and your future begin right now. Your past does not determine your future; you have the power to change your life into what you want it to be.

You have no reason to doubt your worth or potential. God does not doubt you, so your confidence should be paramount. You have only to accept the reality of your real self. In every arena of life, there are those who are successful and those who are unsuccessful. What makes the difference can be summarized in one word. Belief. Belief is one of the most important elements in achieving your life goals. Your beliefs are powerful. They make up the person you will become and influence what you will achieve in life. In order to succeed, you must undoubtedly believe you have the ability to achieve whatever you have set out to do.

What is it that rich, successful, and prosperous people possess that others may not? **They believe in themselves and their God-given abilities**. They respect themselves and earn the respect of others. They have a firm belief in themselves and their mission. No one or anything is going to come between them and their vision.

Take Steve Jobs. He so firmly believed in the Apple brand and his vision for the company, that Apple is currently worth about $750 billion dollars. People will spend hours in line waiting for the new Apple product to be released. It all began with his belief in himself, the Apple brand, and his vision to "Think different."

What is the difference between you and Steve Jobs? You may be thinking a couple billion dollars. He was not born a billionaire; he went out and created a brand that earned him billions of dollars.

> **"Your work is going to fill a large part of your life, and the only way to be truly satisfied is to do what you believe is great work. And the only way to do great work is to love what you do."**
> **Steve Jobs**

In life, people are going to tell you that you cannot achieve the dreams you have set out to accomplish. They will tell you that you do not have the ability, potential, skill, or drive. This is the "crabs in the barrel" mentality. Those people who say you cannot achieve your dreams have to keep you down because your success will eliminate their excuses for not being successful. If you listen to them you will not succeed, you will fail. Do not listen to the cynics and dream killers. Do not listen to those who do not believe in you. Listen to what God says about you and tell yourself that you will succeed and you will achieve what you set out to do. It takes preparation, knowledge, persistence, and work, but you can do anything you aim to do if you believe in yourself. **Be your own #1 fan!**

To develop belief in yourself and your greatest potential of living a prosperous life, you will have to overcome difficulties, doubt, and push yourself beyond any level you may have achieved in the past. You can do it! All the tools you need are available to you.

History is often written by people who believe in a dream so intensely they are willing to commit themselves totally to its realization. You have probably heard it said before, "It is impossible to succeed without believing." In other words, if you want to succeed in life, you must believe in what you are doing. It is called faith, and with it, your possibilities in life are limitless. Without faith, well, the complete opposite is true and it leads you down a pathway of failure every time. Once you come to the complete understanding of the level of abundance God has planned for you, you can rise out of your current dimension and reach a far more prosperous level. No matter where you are now, it is time for you to move to a new dimension of living. God has a divine plan for your life. Begin now to elevate your thoughts to a new dimension, seeking Godly wisdom to guide you into a new level of plenty.

> "For verily I say unto you, That whosoever shall say unto this mountain, Be thou removed, and be thou cast into the sea; and shall not doubt in his heart, but shall believe that those things which he saith shall come to pass; he shall have whatsoever he saith." Mark 11:23

For when you succeed in convincing your subconscious mind that you are wealthy, you believe you deserve to be wealthy, and it feels good to be wealthy, your subconscious mind will automatically seek ways of making your feelings of wealth manifest in material form. **The world as you see it is only a reflection of who you are.**

Be willing to let go of the mental belief patterns and behaviors that have resulted in you living a life that is less than what you have always dreamed. You must look in the mirror when you ask who is responsible for your triumph or let down. As long as you are persistent in your pursuit of your vision, you will continue to grow. You cannot choose the day or time when the vision will come to pass, have faith and believe it will happen on its own time.

Believe with all of your heart that you will do what you were made to do. Once your mind has formed the habit of holding joyous, happy, prosperous pictures, it will not be easy to form the opposite habit. Believe that you are governed by God, and that you are directed by divine guidance. Know that everything you think, say or do that is constructive is done through divine authority. Have faith in your God-given power to be prosperous in life. Focus your efforts on achieving your desires and nothing on earth can keep you from it.

Believe in yourself!

"I firmly believe that any man's finest hour, the greatest fulfillment of all that he holds dear, is the moment when he has worked his heart out in a good cause and lies exhausted on the field of battle—victorious." Vince Lombardi

When you believe you will prosper, you will. If you believe you will win, you will! If you believe you will be wealthy, you will be wealthy. It is evident that you will become like the person you think and believe you are, and achieve only what you think and believe you are capable of. The person who has acquired the power of keeping his mind filled with thoughts of gratitude, abundance, power, confidence, and wealth, which uplift and encourage, has solved one of the great mysteries of life.

When you develop yourself to the point where your belief in yourself is so strong that you know you can accomplish anything you put your mind to, you open the door to unlimited possibilities. You are capable of functioning in a power and might in which nothing can stop you. Even when the going gets rough, you must have belief that your vision will come to pass. You have to continue to use your faith.

Whenever you think of yourself, always hold the image of yourself as you would intend it to be. Do not dwell upon your imperfections or weaknesses, because that will distort your image, but hold tenaciously to the ideal of yourself in your perfection, as the personality God intended you to be. It takes faith and patience to bring these God-given principles to their fullest potential. You must regularly plant your seeds. At first your sowing may look futile. However, there will come a day when the harvest will begin to come up in such abundance that you will have more than enough.

"So you have to be careful of what you believe in; you have to be careful what you think about because your mind is a magnet. And it's going to draw to you whatever it believes, whatever it thinks, whatever it feels, whatever it mentally and inwardly observes." Rev. Ike

You have a purpose in this life. God created you to be the best you. Have the courage to change on the inside; know you will be the greatest God called you to be. Some of the world's most successful individuals throughout time have accomplished what they planned to do, and they believed in themselves even when others did not. Wealthy and successful people understand that there are no shortcuts in life.

Focus more on your desires than on your doubts, and the dream will take care of itself. Your doubts are not as powerful as your desires, unless you make them so. Believe in yourself. This is an important step because without the belief in yourself, you will not have the courage to pursue your goals.

Key points:
- Your belief is your power.
- Be your own #1 fan.
- Do not listen to the cynics and dream killers.
- You will become what you believe you will be.

Key point to practice:
- Visualize and carry yourself with self-confident, and you will not only inspire others with a belief in your ability to achieve your goals, but you will also come to believe yourself. Act as if it is impossible to fail.

<u>Built To Prosper "Belief" Quotes:</u>

"If you wish others to believe in you, you must first convince them that you believe in them."
Harvey Mackay

"Believe and act as if it were impossible to fail."
Charles F. Kettering

"One comes to believe whatever one repeats to oneself sufficiently often, whether the statement be true of false. It comes to be dominating thought in one's mind."
Robert Collier

"Every man must do two things alone; he must do his own believing and his own dying."
Martin Luther

"Every person is the creation of himself, the image of his own thinking and believing. As individuals think and believe, so they are."
Claude M. Bristol

"The strongest single factor in prosperity consciousness is self-esteem: believing you can do it, believing you deserve it, believing you will get it."
Jerry Gillies

"You must understand that seeing is believing, but also know that believing is seeing."
Denis Waitley

CHAPTER V
CREATING AN INSPIRED VISION

CHAPTER V
CREATING AN INSPIRED VISION

"Give us clear vision that we may know where to stand and what to stand for, because unless we stand for something we shall fall for anything." Peter Marshall

A successful person is able to visualize his or her dream and then make it a reality. Do you have a dream you can visualize? Do you have a vision for your life? Or are you functioning on auto pilot aimlessly? **A vision is not seen as a dream, but a reality that has not come into existence**. Your vision should include who you want to be, what you want to do and what you want to have. It is important to know clearly who you are right now and to know who you want to become. This includes your habits, attitudes, and points of view. If you are unclear about yourself, you will be unclear about your future.

When creating a vision, you should know where you are starting and your desired end result. Everything done by human beings first comes into existence by a vision. Only afterward is it translated into the external world. Nothing can be created or accomplished without an idea, a picture, an image, or a sense of the thing first occurring in the mind. Imagine getting in your car with your family, and saying you are going on a family trip and you have no idea where you are going—you just know you are going somewhere. A trip like this would cost you time and money. It is unlikely that you would find a destination you like, if you do not know where you are going.

Your family may have some concerns about you due to your lack of navigation and vision. If you do not have a clear picture of your destination and a precise, detailed map to get there, you will never arrive, no matter how hard you try.

I have heard people whine about being too busy with their daily routine to plan for a better life, much less look ahead, even though they wish their circumstances were better; and we all know wishing gets you no where. I think the truth is not that these people are so busy they cannot plan for a better life but that they are working so hard so they do not have to look at their lives and make necessary changes. They are afraid there is nothing there—no meaning, no purpose, no vision.

They are running on empty. Some time previously, they stopped playing to win and started playing not to lose and now they are losing big time. Fear of failure, peer pressure, and discomfort at the thought of leaving their routine lulled them to settle instead of going for what they truly want. They would rather spend eight to ten hours on a job they do not like and then come home and spend four hours in front of the idiot box to escape their mental prison.

When these people die it will be as though they never lived. In their waning years they will be racked with the pain of regret and haunted by the words "could have", "should have", "if only I would have." You are not going to go down that path; you have come too far to turn back now. Even if you do not achieve all your desires, it is what happens to you as a person in the process of going after your dream that is truly valuable.

> "After you become a millionaire, you can give all of your money away because what's important is not the million dollars; what's important is the person you have become in the process of becoming a millionaire." Jim Rohn

It is about the journey. It is what you become that fulfills you, not what you get. There are two ways you can fail in living your most fulfilling life: not truly believing in your vision, and limiting yourself in what you think you can achieve, basically selling yourself short.

You are Built To Prosper, so there is no time for small thinking. You will never know how far you can go in life until you get up and set sail towards your vision. I urge you to pick the first route to "failure" because it is only in trying to go farther than you think that you can find out how far you can go. **Think big. Aim high. Go strong**.

Are you ready to achieve the unthinkable? Well, begin now to visualize the life you want to live. You will get whatever you visualize and work for. If you keep up this practice and apply it each day of your life, you will find that it will produce the greatness of success and wealth you desire. It is a matter of concentration, preparation, and focusing all your powers upon the law in order to attract your dreams into reality.

Visualization is also the natural process by which the mind communicates deeply buried feelings and beliefs. The importance of making this process conscious is that, without awareness, we usually choose to act according to the way we envision reality around us, not necessarily the way it actually is. Visualize the able, earnest, useful and fruitful prospering person you want to be. It all begins in your mind. **Renew your mind daily**. As you plan to prosper, give yourself the gift of self-discipline. It is a willingness to listen to your inner voice that demands excellence instead of average. Begin by creating your ideal life.

Having a vision might be the most powerful way to keep you focused on what you want in life while keeping you motivated in achieving it. Vision will open up your mind to many possibilities of a greater and brighter future. When you can envision a future that is better, happier, and more productive, you are more likely to make the changes that are necessary for you to reach that reality.

Before you can become the person you dream or before you can have what you want, you must first see yourself in your new life, know how it feels to be what you have decided to be, do, and have.

> "Rule YOUR mind, rule Your WORLD. Have someone else rule your mind, and you'll be a slave in THEIR world."
> Hasheem Francis

You must see yourself as prosperous. You must have a vivid picture in your mind as to what living prosperous means. The mind thinks in pictures. Most people have never had a good mental picture of what being prosperous means or have never stopped to picture themselves as prosperous.

Whatever your intentions are for living a prosperous life, it is time to get it out in the open in as much detail as possible. The time is now, to create your vision. Find yourself somewhere quiet where you can formulate your thoughts. We are going to design the life you desire. Knowing what you want in life is a reward in itself. When you truly know what you want in life it puts you in a different league. It is not always easy to sit down and design your life; we were never taught how to in school. Believe me, if you take the time to visualize what you want and be as specific as possible, those things you desire will draw near to you.

Putting your desires in writing is an important step toward bringing your vision and thoughts into manifestation. Did you know that writing is one of the keys to manifestation?

What Is Your Vision For Your Life?

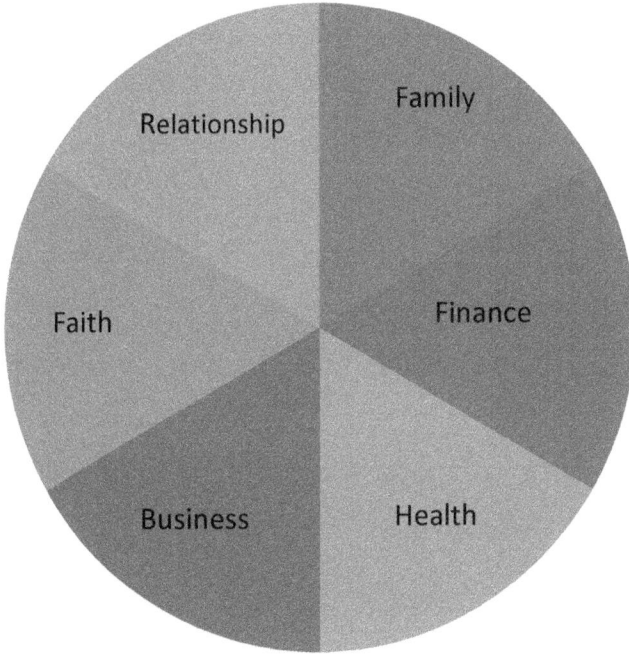

Describe in great detail your vision for each area of your life. Write it in the present tense, as if you have it right now. Write it down in full detail and in living color.

Faith: _____

_____

_____

_____

_____

_____

_____

_____

_____

_____

_____

_____

_____

_____

_____

_____

_____

_____

_____

_____

_____

_____

_____

Family: _____

_____

_____

_____

_____

_____

_____

_____

_____

_____

_____

_____

_____

_____

_____

_____

_____

_____

_____

_____

_____

_____

_____

_____

_____

_____

_____

Health: _____

_____

_____

_____

_____

_____

_____

_____

_____

_____

_____

_____

_____

_____

_____

_____

_____

_____

_____

_____

_____

_____

_____

_____

_____

Career/ Business: _____

_____

_____

_____

_____

_____

_____

_____

_____

_____

_____

_____

_____

_____

_____

_____

_____

_____

_____

_____

_____

_____

_____

_____

Finance: _____

_____

_____

_____

_____

_____

_____

_____

_____

_____

_____

_____

_____

_____

_____

_____

_____

_____

_____

_____

_____

_____

_____

_____

_____

_____

_____

Love/Purpose: _____

_____

_____

_____

_____

_____

_____

_____

_____

_____

_____

_____

_____

_____

_____

_____

_____

_____

_____

_____

_____

_____

_____

_____

_____

_____

_____

_____

Relationships: _____

_____

_____

_____

_____

_____

_____

_____

_____

_____

_____

_____

_____

_____

_____

_____

_____

_____

_____

_____

_____

_____

_____

_____

How would you feel when you are succeeding in life and all your financial needs are taken care of?

_____

_____

_____

_____

_____

_____

_____

_____

_____

_____

_____

_____

_____

_____

_____

_____

_____

_____

_____

_____

_____

_____

_____

_____

Describe what a perfect day would be like for you:

_____

_____

_____

_____

_____

_____

_____

_____

_____

_____

_____

_____

_____

_____

_____

_____

_____

_____

_____

_____

_____

_____

Once you have completed your "vision creation" assignment, feel a sense of accomplishment. Now you know what you want in life and it is written down. You have just designed your life. **Hold this prosperous life vision you just created firmly in your mind, and it will actually happen if you continually affirm it in your thoughts and work diligently to make it happen**.

Always visualize the outcome of the goals as you wish to experience them. The more you can see yourself achieving the goals, the quicker they will become a reality. If you learn to mix emotion along with the visualization, this will accelerate the process as well. Your main purpose is to be absolutely clear about what it is you want, to make a plan to achieve that goal, and then to think about it and work on it every single day. Do not settle for anything less.

Create A Dream Board

> **"To believe in the things you can see and touch is not belief at all. But to believe in the unseen is a triumph and a blessing."**
> **Bob Proctor**

You have invested the time in writing out your desires, but the mind thinks in pictures, so your mind needs visuals. Dream building involves creating a physical representation of what you want to achieve. Your dream board will represent how you visualize the achievement of your goals and your journey toward that achievement.

Look through magazines and find pictures that represent your vision. Get pictures of the beautiful home you plan on living in, get pictures of your family, find pictures that represent success and cut them out and place them on a board. This will be your own personal dream board. If you are married, make this a family activity. **Have some fun with this!**

We currently have five dream boards in our home. (We dream big in my house.) Once you complete your dream board (or boards) place it where you will see it regularly. It will help motivate and inspire you towards achieving your goals.

Back in Chapter II you created twenty-one positive affirmations. Add these affirmations to your dream board. In time, you will become a more definite, positive, focused, optimistic, creative, and determined person. The more you become, the more you will begin to activate all of your mind's power and organize all the mental laws to work on your behalf. You will be achieving at a higher level than you ever have before.

Key points:

- Think big, there is no room for small thinking.
- Enjoy the process in developing your vision.
- Practice visualizing your goals daily.
- Your mind thinks in pictures. Dream big.

Key points to practice:

- Focus on your vision daily.
- Review your written vision once a day.

Built To Prosper "Vision" Quotes

"Formulate and stamp indelibly on your mind a mental picture of yourself as succeeding. Hold this picture tenaciously. Never permit it to fade. Your mind will seek to develop the picture."
Norman Vincent Peal

"Visualize this thing you want. See it, feel it, believe in it. Make your mental blueprint and begin."
Robert Collier

"Cherish your visions and your dreams, as they are the children of your soul, the blueprints of your ultimate achievements."
Napoleon Hill

"The most pathetic person in the world is someone who has sight, but has no vision."
Helen Keller

"Capital isn't scarce; vision is."
Sam Walton

"To believe in the things you can see and touch is no belief at all. But to believe in the unseen is both a triumph and a blessing."
Bob Proctor

"I would give all the wealth of the world, and all the deeds of all the heroes, for one true vision."
Henry David Thoreau

CHAPTER VI

DECIDE OR BE CONFORMED

CHAPTER VI
DECIDE OR BE CONFORMED

> "If you want to become a leader in your business, stay hungry and be productive. No matter what obstacles you face, learn to keep moving forward until you succeed."
> **Hasheem Francis**

You do not have a problem to solve, you simply have a decision to make. Our decisions set the course of our lives. If you had a choice to continue down your current path and live the exact life you are living right now, or to make a decision that would change everything right now, which would you choose? **Until a decision is made and acted upon, nothing happens**.

No one can decide for you. If you want to control the direction of your life, you must develop the habit of making good decisions. Making wise decisions is one of life's greatest challenges. It is not what you do once in a while that has an impact on the direction of your life, it is what you do consistently. **Decide today that you are not going to live in mediocrity.**

For you to get the results you desire in life, it is imperative to decide what results you are committed to and know specifically how these results will change your life. It is critical to decide what kind of person you are committed to becoming. Get clear about what you want to be, do, and have and what your life will be like after you accomplish this.

With clarity you will find it becomes easier to make the kind of decisions that will move you in the direction you desire. Our past decisions cause the circumstances we face in life. The future events we may experience depend upon the kind of decisions we make today.

Life is made up of little and big decisions and how a man or woman decides determine the course of his or her life. Successful people know how to make decisions. If you do not learn how to make good decisions, you will continue to have the kind of results you had up until now. Deciding creates the purpose; it gives you a goal, a reason to do what you do. Once a decision is made, carrying it out becomes a matter of will, courage, and dedication.

> **"Decision is born of courage and courage springs forth from faith in self and in the God power within." Claude M. Bristol**

Make a decision today to develop yourself to the point where you can achieve your personal goals and become everything you are capable of becoming. Be diligent in your decisions, write your goals down and make sure you look at them every day, then ponder ways you can possibly achieve these goals. Determine exactly what you want to be able to do. Decide who you want to become. Describe exactly what you will look like when you become successful in your personal life and business. Your decision to live a prosperous life is not an overnight success. **There is some work that is required**.

No matter what difficulties may arise, no matter how much harder your work may be than you anticipated, do not waiver or turn back. Those who think life is not just and whine and complain about how life is so unfair are simply increasing their own troubles. Until that person realizes that the cause of all his troubles are due to the decisions he made in life, he cannot make the necessary changes that would lead him towards a life of success. His thoughts, ideals, and attitude about life must all become transformed. The Apostle Paul stated, "Be ye transformed by the renewing of your mind."

Set your face toward your goals; never permit anyone or anything to undermine your destiny. Saturate your mind with thoughts of success, wealth, health, and prosperity. You can become who you want and have what you desire if you make the decision to think on it. It may take some time before your desires manifest physically in your life, but be patient—you will not be denied. Most people have already decided to follow the masses.

These people are being conformed. It is easy to do what everyone else is doing. It is easy to sit in front of a television ("Tell You Their Vision"), for three hours and not work on building a relationship with your spouse or children. It is easy to not go to the gym and work out; it is very easy for a college student to put off doing an important research paper and go party with their friends. I know this because I have done it myself. My favorite line was if everyone else is "not" doing it, why should I? My old friends were not reading great books like *Think and Grow Rich*, *The 21 Irrefutable Laws of Leadership*, or *Rich Dad, Poor Dad*.

The day I decided to change my way of thinking was the day I met my wife, Deborah. I think it is appropriate to share the story of how I met her. I remember the day: November 23, 1998. It was a Monday; I had the day off from work. At the time I was working as a security guard making $6.15 hour. What was I thinking risking my life for $6.15?

The reason I remember this day is that it was my day of ultimate disgust. I was disgusted with my life; I was a grown man living with my mother, sleeping on a bunk bed. I was working at a job where there was no opportunity for growth, just an extra $0.25 raise after 2 years of working. I was definitely tired of playing the dating game. So I "decided" that day I was going change my life. I enrolled in a Business School that day. I also decided I was going to get a dog as my companion, because I heard a dog is a man's best friend, and I needed a new friend.

> **"Once you make a decision, the universe conspires to make it happen." Ralph Waldo Emerson**

That day, I went to the local neighborhood pet store and saw a nice looking brown German Sheppard in the window that caught my eye, so I went in to ask for the price of my new best friend. When I turned to walk to show the store owner the dog I was referring to, this beautiful woman was standing there. Her teeth were pearly white—she had a smile that would stop traffic. It sure stopped me. Life can throw a curve ball sometimes: I went to get a companion and came out with a beautiful, loving, and supportive wife (I did not ask her to marry me that day, even though I wanted to). I am grateful I made that decision, because my life has been a blessing ever since. **That is how life happens: when you make a decision and take action, life has a funny way of rewarding you.**

Life is perfectly just and rewards every person according to their work. I could have decided to stay home that day and not enroll in Business School or go to the pet store. If I never acted on my decision, I would not have met the most wonderful woman that God created just for me. I had to put action behind my decision.

People make decisions every day, but they never act on them. They sit in front of the television, or listen to those who do not have a vision for their own life and they become conformed to their environment. I have seen this happen time and time again; people with such great talent just waste their lives away. They decide to conform to the ways of the world.

In order to gain control over your life, you must take your power back and learn how to allow yourself to be what you have envisioned. You are responsible for ruling your own actions and decisions. To make consistently good decisions, and take the right action when needed, requires character and self-discipline.

Society has been programmed to be dependent, not independent. Many believe and have decided that they will gain wealth through dependency, not independence. They are seeking handouts not hand ups.

We are taught to depend on the government to take care of us when we get old through a social security check. The masses are taught to keep working a job they hate just for a steady paycheck. Then you have those that are hoping someday to win the lotto. This is not independent thinking, because the power belongs to that which you depend on. Who sold us on that plan?

If you read this far, I know you will make the wise decision and not be conformed. It is your life to live and make count. Wealth and great prosperity await you. **Decide today that you will be all that God created you to be**. Venture out. Refuse to stay in the valley of mediocrity.

Key points:
- Make the decision to be prosperous and act on it.
- Do not be conformed by the negative opinions of other people.
- It is your life to live, make it count.

Built To Prosper "Decision" Quotes:

"Once you make a decision, the universe conspires to make it happen."
Ralph Waldo Emerson

"Be willing to make decisions. That's the most important quality in a good leader. Don't fall victim to what I call the ready aim-aim syndrome. You must be willing to fire."
T. Boone Pickens

"Every choice you make has an end result."
Zig Ziglar

"I found every single successful person I've ever spoken to had a turning point. The turning point was when they made a clear, specific unequivocal decision that they were not going to live like this anymore; they were going to achieve success. Some people make that decision at fifteen and some people make it at fifty, and most people never make it all."
Brian Tracy

"Using the power of decision gives you the capacity to get past any excuse to change any and every part of your life in an instant."
Anthony Robbins

"Everything is something you decide to do, and there is nothing you have to do."
Denis Waitley

"The most difficult thing is the decision to act, the rest is merely tenacity. The fears are paper tigers. You can do anything you decide to do. You can act to change and control your life; and the procedure, the process is its own reward."
Amelia Earhart

CHAPTER VII

ARE YOU COMMITTED TO THE CAUSE?

CHAPTER VII
ARE YOU COMMITTED TO THE CAUSE?

> "There are only two options regarding commitment. You're either in or out. There's no such thing as a life in-between."
> **Pat Riley**

I have created a prosperous life personally and have observed many people who have reached this level and beyond. My observation is there is nothing magical about it; it is a choice of all-out commitment. **Prosperity, success, or wealth does not necessarily go to the most talented or gifted, but to those who are the most committed**.

The difference between average living and prosperous living is a matter of commitment. Are you committed to creating a life filled with prosperity? Those that have a high prosperity consciousness simply make commitments to achieve greater goals. Fear of the unknown is one of the greatest obstacles you will face when you are traveling on the journey towards a prosperous life. **A worthwhile goal can never be achieved without encountering failures, criticism, obstacles and roadblocks**.

Your greatness will be molded and measured by the mountains you choose to conquer. And there will be some mountains you will definitely need to overcome, such as fear of failure and any limiting beliefs that may be holding you back from achieving your desired life. Worthwhile goals are always found on the top of rugged mountains, never on valley floors. **You must overcome your fear of failure in**

order to achieve your dreams. Fear of failure is the enemy of your success. Failure is not a disaster; it is an event in which you did not achieve your desired outcome. You can learn more from your failure than you can from your success, it can make you wiser. If you read the autobiography of anyone who has achieved great success you will see that person had to overcome some great failures to achieve his dreams. Many successful people had to overcome bankruptcy, failed marriages, and drug habits.

Failure became their greatest teacher and mentor. Every person has within them the ability to accomplish great things because of their ability to learn, improve, emulate and change. Change demands self-discipline, so you must command yourself and make yourself do what needs to be done. If you desire a better life than what you have now, you must learn to overcome all fears and obstacles that stand in your way. Fear can be a tyrannical dictator that drastically limits or even destroys your hopes and dreams. Many people may experience fear when they are moving outside of their comfort zone. **Remember: There is no wealth inside the comfort zone**. Step outside of what has become comfortable and familiar. You must risk losing control in order to push yourself into the outer limits of your abilities. It is the way to a prosperous life.

People who see themselves as failures, lacking, or have a low self esteem will eventually fail regardless of their best efforts to succeed, while people who see themselves as prosperous, successful, and confident will eventually create the life they desire regardless of how many mountains they may have to climb or run through. They are committed to the process.

> **"If you want something, you have to take action. Plan, learn and absorb as much as you want, but without action, you will never get to where you want to be." Hasheem Francis**

I would like to share a story with you about commitment. When I was living in New York City a couple of years ago, we experienced a severe snow storm. There was about two feet of snow on the ground. I had an event that evening I committed to and needed a haircut. (I get paid to look good.) I called my barber, whose shop was about two miles from my home. He was a committed business owner, so I knew his shop would be open. The New York City buses were not running and the cab services were not available, so I decided to walk the two miles. Walking the two miles in two feet of snow was not the issue. I had a dilemma: my nephew, who was seven years old at the time, wanted to spend time with me, so I decided to take him with me. I explained to him that it was going to be a long walk and he has to dress warm. He was a child so he thought it would be fun.

We walked the two miles to the barber shop without any problems and I must admit it was fun, I felt like a kid again. I got my haircut, and my nephew and I left the barbershop and we began our journey back home. Ten minutes in, my nephew said his feet were getting cold. My first thought was, "Please let a bus appear so I can get this kid home safely," but instead of waiting for a bus that would never appear, I told him, "Let's keep walking." As we continued to walk, I heard him moan, so I started to panic. I had at least a mile and a half to walk and there was no bus in sight. I had a decision to make and needed to decide fast. So, I carried my nephew on my neck and covered his feet with my hands to keep them warm. I walked that mile and a half. I was committed to getting him and me home.

My nephew, who is a teenager now, always reminds me of that story. I keep this story close to my heart so anytime I get a little weary I remember that day. **I learned that anytime you are committed to achieving a particular goal, you must stay the course no matter what**. There was no turning back, I had to go forward, and most importantly, no one gets left behind on my watch.

Those who succeed in their undertakings are those who set their faces toward their goal, and with unwavering conviction, affirm and reaffirm their confidence in their ability to reach it. God did not make us to be a failure. He made us to be and to live prosperously. Expect the best. You must put your whole heart into what you want to accomplish. People are defeated in life not because they lack ability, but because they lack faith in their abilities.

> "Persistence is the quality that causes you to arise, when once you have been knocked down by temporary failure, and to continue your pursuit of a given desire or object. It is the quality that gives you courage and faith to keep on trying in the face of any and all obstacles that may confront you."
> Napoleon Hill

If you are a person who wants to win in every aspect of your life, being committed to the process must be ingrained in your subconscious mind. A major key to success in life, to getting whatever you really seek, is to have the mindset of "I will, until…" Whatever you are going to do, give it your all. Hold nothing back. I have created the mindset **"I will consistently persist until I achieve my desired outcome."** What is your mindset about keeping commitments and being persistent in achieving your desires? We all have the same twenty-four hours in a day. Once you make the commitment to make the necessary changes in life, distractions will come, and they will come by the truckload. The difference between those who achieve success and those who do not is that those who are successful know how to make the most of their twenty-four hours.

No one has complete control over their daily life; someone or something always seems to be pulling us in many directions. But you must develop the habit of saying no to things that waste time and are not priorities.

One way to use your time wisely is to cut down on activities that do not move you forward toward your goal. **To effectively manage yourself within time, you need to set goals. When you know where you are going, you can then figure out what exactly needs to be done and in what order**. Without proper goal setting, you will waste your time on confusing and conflicting priorities. People tend to neglect goal setting because it requires time and effort. What they fail to consider is that a little time and effort put in now saves an enormous amount of time, effort, and frustration in the future.

Learn to say no to tasks and people that are a distraction. This is not being selfish, this is called being focused and committed. Planning helps you increase your useful time. When you have a plan and it is written on paper, it will more than likely keep you committed, and it will be your blueprint on how to get from where you are to where you desire to be. Prioritizing what needs to be done is especially important. Without it, you may work hard, but you will not achieve the results you desire because what you are working on is not of strategic importance. Most people have a "to do" list of some sort. The problem with many of these lists is they are just a list of activities that need to get done. There is no rhyme or reason to the list and, because of this, the work they do is just as unstructured. To work efficiently, you need to work on the most important, highest-value tasks.

My business partners and I meet once a month to discuss the company's monthly goals and review our annual goals. One person is assigned to keep record of our discussions. We address any new product ideas or services we intend to bring to the market and we also discuss each team member's monthly goals. At the end of the meeting we all receive an email with everything we discussed. Now it is each team member's responsibility to include their goals in their daily or monthly planner. So when the team meets at the beginning of the following month, we can go over our goals, and if someone has not achieved a goal, we can always go back to the team member's daily activity to see if the person was utilizing his or her time effectively.

Take Responsibility

As you go on this journey, you must take responsibility for your life. By taking responsibility for your life, you have control. You no longer live a life of blame. Those that live a life of blame live in a mental prison; they give all their power to outside circumstances. Those circumstances hold the key to their freedom. **If you learn to fully accept the responsibility for where you are right now despite your past mistakes, you will be empowered by one of the foundational principles of success**. The prosperous spirit within you cannot be honed or harnessed if you cannot accept total responsibility for your life. You see, if you are stuck in the blame mode, you cannot get to where you want to go.

Those that take responsibility for the results in their life stick with their vision and if the actions they are implementing are not getting them the results they desire, they become flexible. They are not afraid of change. They give it their all. On your journey you will face unexpected situations, but you must stay the course. I never met or read about anyone who has achieved great success that has not come up against some sort of opposition. It is part of the development process. Great success does not come easy. **It takes commitment and sacrifice, and the more ambitious the goal, the greater the sacrifice**.

Do you know what it is you want to do? What career path do you want to take? What brings you joy? You need to know what you want to do, why you want to do it and have a plan of action on how to go about achieving your goals. You need to know the benefits of taking action and the negative consequences for not taking action. Acquiring clarity and increasing effectiveness will accelerate your success.

Most people get excited about their dreams and goals in the infant stages of planning, but once any setbacks come, they quit. This is the main reason why most successful people say it is lonely at the top and crowded at the bottom. Some people are not committed; they will not participate in their own rescue. It simply takes too much commitment and sacrifice to achieve a great level of success. I know I will probably lose a couple of readers with that last statement. Some people are afraid of these two words: commitment and sacrifice. Many failed marriages and business opportunities come from the lack of understanding of these two words. **In order to achieve your goals in life, it will take commitment, sacrifice, perseverance, and discipline.** Perseverance is the ability to keep going despite the circumstances.

People that live a life of blame give up easily, but those that take responsibility stay the course. They focus on the things that are important. If they are not sure, they seek counsel from those who are in their area of need. When seeking counsel, you must put your pride aside and not be afraid to ask for guidance.

When you take responsibility for the results you get in life, you will no longer settle for mediocrity. Your standards will change, and you will begin to set higher aims. The situations you used to tolerate are no longer acceptable. Determine the specific habits and behaviors you will need to practice every day to become the person you want to become. **These could include: determination, focus, persistence, working smart, and studiousness.**

"The kind of commitment I find among the best performers across virtually every field is a single-minded passion for what they do, an unwavering desire for excellence in the way they think and the way they work. Genuine confidence is what launches you out of bed in the morning, and through your day with a spring in your step." Jim Collins

Are You Committed?

Exercise: **Explain your new mindset on your commitment to your goals.** Write it out, post it all around your home, put it in your car, and tape it on your bathroom mirrors. Say it to yourself while you are looking directly into the mirror, face-to-face with yourself. It may feel uncomfortable at first, but you now know staying within a comfort zone will keep you broke and unfulfilled.

_____

_____

_____

_____

_____

_____

_____

Key points:
- Be committed to your vision, regardless of the circumstances.
- Great success does not come easy.
- Be flexible in pursuit of your goals.
- Take responsibility for your results.

Built To Prosper "Commitment" Quotes:

"Anyone can dabble, but once you've made that commitment, your blood has that particular thing in it, and it's very hard for people to stop you."
Anonymous

"If you are truly flexible and go until... there is really very little you can't accomplish in your lifetime."
Anthony Robbins

"Making your mark on the world is hard. If it were easy, everybody would do it. But it's not. It takes patience, it takes commitment, and it comes with plenty of failure along the way. The real test is not whether you avoid this failure, because you won't. It's whether you let it harden or shame you into inaction, or whether you learn from it; and you choose to persevere."
Barack Obama

"The quality of a person's life is in direct proportion to their commitment to excellence, regardless of their chosen field of endeavor."
Vincent Lombardi

"There's no scarcity of opportunity to make a living at what you love. There is only a scarcity of resolve to make it happen."
Wayne Dyer

"It was character that got us out of bed, commitment that moved us into action, and discipline that enabled us to follow through."
Zig Ziglar

"Productivity is never an accident. It is always the result of a commitment to excellence, intelligent planning, and focused effort."
Paul J. Meyer

CHAPTER VIII

CREATING YOUR CIRCLE OF TRUST

CHAPTER VIII
CREATING YOUR CIRCLE OF TRUST

"Don't join the easy crowd; YOU won't GROW. Connect with people who have something of value to share with you."
Hasheem Francis

I f you want to be successful in life, you need a team of like-minded individuals who are not afraid to hold you accountable. Each of us has groups of people with whom we surround ourselves. We have our business associates, we have our friends, and we have our family members. Many times these people have a much greater influence on us than we might think. Many people do not achieve their desired success because of the people they have allow in their circle.

The individuals we allow in our circle can either propel us towards success or be a hindrance. To succeed in life, you have to surround yourself with people who believe in your success and want you to succeed. Your inner circle needs to be part of your success.

My mentor advised me to choose my friends and business partners wisely. To be honest I did not listen at first, because I thought I knew who my real friends were. Little did I know, I was in for a surprise.

When I started my first company, I thought all my friends would be happy for my success and come support my endeavors. The people I thought would be with me through thick and thin became the people who were not happy for my success in the end.

Someone once told me if you want to see who your true friends are, become successful or have a financial hardship. Everyone is not going to applaud your success. This can be difficult for those who are not emotionally strong or those who value other people's opinion above their own.

> "Keep away from those who try to belittle your ambitions. Small people always do that, but the really great make you believe that you too can become great." Mark Twain

Having the right people around you is critical to your success. To pursue success effectively you must build supportive relationships that will help you work toward your goals. No one ever achieved success on his or her own. It is not wise to try and do it by yourself. Everyone needs some sort of help; Jesus recruited twelve disciples to help spread his message. **You can achieve infinitely more with partners than you ever could by yourself. Partnering is the key to removing the limits of your limiting resources. It multiplies your own potential**.

To build those relationships, you need to learn to trust others and they must trust you in turn. No person has ever possessed enough resources—meaning time, talent, and money—to achieve extraordinary success on their own. We all need a team. Every person who has ever achieved extraordinary success, whether personally or professionally, has done it with a great deal of help from others. When you understand that you do not have all the necessary resources to achieve your dreams, it forces you to look for mentors who are rich in knowledge and resources.

You may have the talent or ideas for a new business venture, but you may lack the time or the money to effectively pursue this business venture. Therefore, you can partner with someone who may have the time and partner with someone else who may have the money for investment capital. **You can get more done with a team than you can on your own.**

Warning: There will always be those who say something cannot be done, or worse, that you cannot do it. Someone once told me that there are only a few negative people in the world, and they just travel around more frequently, ending up wherever you are. To fulfill your desires it will require an unwavering commitment to your goals that cannot be shaken by the negative, often uneducated and misinformed, comments of others. You must at all cost, watch who you allow in your trusted circle. Many will be a distraction and you will have to limit your time with them as you travel on your journey.

Relationship is about giving, not getting. This is where I think most people make the biggest mistakes in their relationships. People are always looking at what they are getting out of the relationship instead of what they are giving to it. If you go into relationships wanting to get rather than give you will always lose. No relationship will work well if either party does not do what they promise to do.

The best relationships that survive and succeed are those in which each person takes responsibility and follows through on the commitment. Building good quality relationships takes time and is something you constantly have to work at if you want the relationship to be meaningful. Relationships do not just happen you need to learn to understand people and their basic need to have great relationships. You basically need to know how to deal with people and understand that all the same rules apply whether you are close to the person or not.

If you are having trouble building quality relationships, I highly recommend you read Dale Carnegie's **How to Win Friends and Influence People.** This book has done wonders for me and my business. I actually read this book once a year because I have learned that to have quality relationships, I must continue to learn what it takes to sustain these relationships. For example, my wife knows I love her. Yes, she should know this, but not showing my love by complimenting her, taking walks holding her hand, or remembering our anniversary would definitely affect my marriage, and not in a positive way.

The same goes with my children; they are a part of my inner circle. I need to remember to compliment them. They know I love them; I have been feeding them and providing for their needs all these years. I value my relationship with my family, friends, and business partners, so I must continue to grow, not just for them, but for myself. When you develop your circle of trust, select members that would hold you accountable and not allow you to slack off from your commitments, and expect the same from them.

Select leaders who do not give less than their best. Make sure they take pride in being in your circle, only accept standards of excellence, and never allow anyone to corrupt these standards. If you associate with negative people, you tend to become negative. If you keep company with a con artist or a thief, people will soon begin to associate you with these attributes. The proverb states, "birds of a feather flock together." Start spending time with people who are moving towards success. Look for people who are goal-oriented, motivated, and career minded. Soon you will start adapting to that type of behavior.

Remember, success leaves clues, so the most effective way to achieve success is to associate with other successful people. If you want to be relentless, associate with relentless people. If want to be wealthy, associate with wealthy people to develop rich ideas. Choosing your associates is important because over the course of time, people become like the people with whom they associate. If you surround yourself with positive thinking people, you will begin to see the benefits of positive thinking working in your life.

As you begin to make the necessary changes and commitment to prospering and being successful, you are going to have to build a team. Author Napoleon Hill called this having a "mastermind" group.

I sought out wealthy people who achieved success and were willing to share their principles with me so I could achieve what I wanted in life. To my surprise, there were many successful people who were willing to take the time to mentor me. They saw the fire in my eyes, and I was serious about achieving my goals. I truly valued their time, so I made the most of it. **Key:** If someone is willing to spend time with you and mentor you, make sure you respect their time.

Comparison

Do you constantly compare yourself to others? Comparing ourselves to others does more harm to a relationship than good. No one likes to be around a person who is always trying to one-up them. You remodel your kitchen and they go and buy a new house. You have finger food at your party and they go and hire a personal chef for their party. Comparison does not motivate you to do more or be better; instead it makes you feel like you will never be good enough. When people compare themselves in an attempt to measure their own success, they set themselves up for nothing more than mediocrity.

Using others as your yardstick places a limit on your success. Most people do not need to worry about other people being in competition with them. Other people are not the reason that they fail at achieving their life goals. Rather, they disqualify themselves with a lack of discipline, direction, and focus.

People that have a fear of success tend to separate themselves from those that are successful, because those who dare to risk and achieve remind them of what they are not doing. They usually condemn those that are successful to avoid this pain. Only when you are able to truly appreciate and enjoy others' success are you setting up the right mental attitude to be successful yourself.

Each time we sincerely applaud others for their achievements, we can rest assured our own success is coming closer because our consciousness is focused on it.

Few people dare to compare themselves to the truly successful, and those who do usually look to successful people as a source of inspiration. People who lack self-confidence can find it difficult to become successful.

Many people lack self-confidence and are unwilling to set their aims higher for fear of failing. This can sometimes stem from the people who are discouraging them because they feel their goals and life choices are unrealistic. It may be that friends and family do not approve, so they use ridicule to prevent their loved one from making what they feel is a mistake.

If you read the autobiographies or biographies of some of the world's most successful people, you will see they did not let their circumstances or environment determine their outcome. "Our success, or lack of it, can be influenced by the people with whom we associate." If you associate with people who are successful or determined to be successful, you will pattern your actions accordingly.

If you aspire to be successful in life, you must be able to build and maintain meaningful relationships. You must become someone who is able to inspire and develop others, a person of loyalty, respect, and trust. And most importantly you must choose your relationships wisely. As you consider your definition of prosperity, remember that your success will ultimately be based on the quality of relationships you develop with other successful people.

Create relationships with people who will hold you accountable and encourage you on the path to your goals. Find ways to spend more time with people who love to help and build others to their full potential. Only share your vision with people who will support you, not those who will respond with cynicism or indifference.

If you want to start a business, for instance, subscribe to business magazines and start befriending those who already have successful businesses. You will find that their attitude is infectious, and you will start believing that you can be successful in business too. Being around people who have created successful businesses can be extremely motivating. A great place to meet other business owners is through your local chamber of commerce or a trade association.

Do whatever it takes to create relationships with people who will hold you accountable and help you keep your commitments.

Write out the 10 qualities you value in a relationship. *Focus on what you want in a relationship, not on what you do not want.*

1. _____

2. _____

3. _____

4. _____

5. _____

6. _____

7. _____

8. _____

9. _____

10. _____

Do You Have A Mentor?

Make a list of five individuals who you would consider or would like to be a mentor to you for each area of life. It can be someone from your local community or someone you admire.

Leadership Mentors

1._____

2._____

3._____

4._____

5._____

Spiritual Mentors

1._____

2._____

3._____

4._____

5._____

Family Mentors

1._____

2._____

3._____

4._____

5._____

Health Mentors

1._____

2._____

3._____

4._____

5._____

Financial Mentors

1._____

2._____

3._____

4._____

5._____

Relationship Mentors

1._____

2._____

3._____

4._____

5._____

Business Mentors

1._____

2._____

3._____

4._____

5._____

"One piece of log creates a small fire, adequate to warm you up. Add just a few more pieces to blast an immense bonfire, large enough to warm up your entire circle of friends; needless to say that individuality counts, but team work dynamites."
Master Jin Kwon

Having mentors is important to your success. Many have already traveled the road you may be on. I remember the words from my mentor, "Always learn from other people's mistakes and successes. It will save you time and money." Through my experiences in life, I have seen people who have dreamed big dreams but failed to live them out due to the people they surrounded themselves with. I learned early that everyone is not going to arrive at the same destination with you. The people that may have started with you may not be the same ones that finish with you. There is going to be some new faces and places as you grow and develop. Although this can be difficult for some people, you also need to remove the negative people from your life. My mentor said he could see my future just by looking at the five people with whom I spend the most time.

To be honest I did not like what I saw. I had to change my circle of friends. It was not that they were bad people; we were just headed in two different directions in life. My desire was to be a business owner and not live from paycheck to paycheck. I wanted to travel and meet new people. It was when I started to change my associations and got around people who wanted or had successful businesses that my thinking began to expand. And once your thinking expands it is difficult to do things the same. One of the reasons people fail to start their own businesses, for instance, is that they spend most of their time associating with people who do not have a vision for their life. **Mindsets are contagious, so spend your time with people whose mindset is worth catching.**

Key points:

- Build relationships with people who can help and will encourage you as you achieve goals.
- Spend more time with other successful people. Mindsets are contagious.
- Everyone is not going to be happy for your success. Separate from those who do not believe in your vision.
- Find mentors who achieved what you desire and ask to be mentored by them.
- Applaud other people's success.

<u>Built To Prosper "Circle of Trust" Quotes:</u>

"It is of practical value to learn to like yourself. Since you must spend so much time with yourself you might as well get some satisfaction out of the relationship."
Norman Vincent Peale

"You can buy a person's hands but you can't buy his heart. His heart is where his enthusiasm, his loyalty is."
Stephen Covey

"If we are together nothing is impossible. If we are divided all will fail."
Winston Churchill

"I really want people to know that I've worked hard to get to where I am today...this didn't just happen overnight. I started in business over twenty-five years ago and I have found a way to build on what I've learned through every partnership and opportunity."
Magic Johnson

"You need to surround yourself with quality human beings that are intelligent and have a vision."
Vince McMahon

"People who have good relationships at home are more effective in the marketplace."
Zig Ziglar

"The quality of your life is the quality of your relationships."
Anthony Robbins

CHAPTER IX

I SHALL HAVE WHAT I DESIRE

CHAPTER IX
I SHALL HAVE WHAT I DESIRE

"If you are bored with life—if you do not get up every morning with a burning desire to do things—you do not have enough goals." Lou Holtz

In the previous chapters of this book, we focused on your thoughts, beliefs, attitude, vision, decisions, commitment, and your circle of trust. These are the key components in building a prosperous life, but it takes a burning desire to bring manifestation of prosperity into your life.

Your desire must be stronger than your circumstances. When my business partners and I first built our investment business, we were strapped for cash in the beginning stages as a company. Any cash flow we received, we reinvested it back into the business, and we knew that all the sacrifices we made were going to pay off. Some of the executives, including myself, did not take a salary for the first two years. Our desire for building a successful company was much greater than our short term cash flow circumstances.

We knew what we wanted, we created the vision, we developed the plan, and we took action. All these things are fine and well, but if we did not have the desire that was strong enough to get us through the rough periods, we would have given up in the earlier stages.

So I understand and know what it is like to face unfavorable circumstances in business and in life, and I would not trade any of those situations for anything. **The tough times made me stronger; they gave me something that could not be bought or sold, and that is an unquenchable desire to see my dreams and goals come to pass**. My mentor expressed to me, "When you make the decision to be successful, just be prepared for a butt kicking." He did not put it in those exact same words; I will keep it PG for the mature audience.

Got Desire?

Desire is like gas in the engine, and what good is a car without gas? Without the gas you will be stuck in the garage or break down on the side of the road. It will be the same in life if you do not have the desire to achieve your goals. No lukewarm effort or indifferent ambition ever accomplished anything. Many people make halfhearted efforts in life; their resolutions are spineless, and there is no backbone in their endeavor, no grit in their ambition. Desire is a powerful force of attraction that acts like a magnet, drawing what we want to us.

People who live ordinary, mundane lives have not gotten in touch with their true desires. At some point in life they just gave up or stopped dreaming all together. In order to achieve great things in life or have extraordinary relationships, or a healthy body, you must have a burning desire. Oh yes, if you want a healthy body, you must have the desire to do what is necessary to develop and maintain it.

Whatever we long for, struggle for, and hold persistently in the mind, we tend to become, in exact proportion to the intensity and persistency of the thought. **Life gives us exactly what we desire. Nothing more, nothing less**. By every thought and every feeling growing out of your mind, you have created the environment in which you now live. **Whether the environment is prosperous or lacking, large or small, successful or failing, you and you alone are responsible.**

Earl Nightingale stated in his bestselling audio program *The Strangest Secret*, "Your returns in life are exactly what you gave." There is a huge difference between living a positive, productive life and barely existing or surviving. How and why we live is much more important than simply living. **It should come as no surprise that more often than not, the people who end up being successful in life are the ones who know exactly what they want and they take the time to write their goals and focus on their desires while taking action daily to achieve their goals.**

What do you desire in life?

_____

_____

_____

_____

_____

_____

_____

_____

_____

_____

_____

_____

_____

_____

_____

_____

_____

_____

_____

When you write your goals, you are putting them in visible form. Up until you actually write your goals, it was just a notion in your mind. Once written, you can now see them, you can read over them and make adjustments where needed. You can also review them on a regular basis. It would be most helpful to write your goals on an index card, keep it with you, and look at it at least four times a day. The reason behind this method is the more you visualize and know exactly what you want, the more you tend to move toward those things in life.

> **"When you discover your mission, you will feel its demand. It will fill you with enthusiasm and a burning desire to get to work on it." W. Clement Stone**

People with goals know exactly where they are going. Goal-oriented people make up their minds about exactly what they want and keep their eyes and enthusiasm on that goal until it becomes a reality in their lives. Be intentional about setting and achieving your goals. Do this every day and it will become a habit that will lead you continuously toward them. These goals must be consistent with your values; we discussed this in the previous chapter. Your goals have to be consistent with what you believe to be true, valuable, and important. Success and true happiness is when your desires are in line with your life values and purpose. **You must always evaluate what you truly want in life because sometimes your desires may lead you away from your values if you are not mindful of them.**

Are You Dressed For Success?

You are probably saying, what does my style of dress have to do with success? People tend to treat you according to the manner in which you are dressed. I have noticed when I am dressed in a t-shirt and shorts most people treat me differently from when I am dressed in a suit. Do I think this is fair? No, but I have come to realize that we live in a world where we are judged by our appearance. We are always judging books by their cover. Do I feel like putting on a suit all the time? No. It takes time to look good. There are days when I have to go to a business meeting and I do not feel like getting dressed. But I know if I show up to the meeting looking any other way than my best, I will more than likely not get the same treatment and results as if I came suited up. When I first learned about dressing for success, I asked some successful business men about different types of suits, and the best advice I got was, "do not buy cheap suits." Did I listen? No. At that time I did not believe I should be spending more than $69.00 for a suit. Do not laugh, yes, you read it right, $69.00 for suit. I thought I was hot stuff in my $69.00 polyester suit.

I wore that suit until it was out of style. I probably would have kept that suit until that infamous day. This was my only suit at the time, so needless to say I wore it a lot. Well one day as I was preparing to put on that suit, I stood in front of the mirror to check how good I looked. It was a beautiful day and the sun was shining, when I looked in the mirror I noticed my suit had iron prints all over it, from me ironing it every week. This was my first lesson in clothing: do not buy cheap polyester suits. Polyester wears faster, and produces shiny spots. Now I know why people were laughing at me when they saw me in that suit. (Pardon me, I just had another flashback.) Do you think after this experience I listened to the businessmen who told me to buy an all-wool suit? Absolutely...not.

I was in the business of being conservative with my money (cheap), I was watching my cash flow, and so I went out and brought not one, but two $79.00 polyester suits. I thought I was like Donald Trump with the $10.00 increase in my suit purchase, styling and profiling. Did things change because I spent $10.00 more on the suits? Oh no, I just ended up with two cheap polyester suits with iron prints on them. Take it from me, it may cost more for all wool suits, but it is well worth the investment. Also you do not look prosperous walking around with a cheap polyester suit with shiny iron prints on it. You will never get a second chance to make a first impression. Evaluate yourself to determine if you are presenting yourself in the best light. Take an objective look. Does your look and dress portray success? Maybe it is time for a make-over and not a $69.00 makeover. When you look good, you will feel better about yourself and your attitude will exude confidence. Confidence attracts success, and believe me, you cannot be confident walking around with a polyester suit with iron prints all over it. **Key: Buy quality clothing. They will last longer and look better in the long run.**

One of the most common complaints I have heard from people over the years is that in the pursuit of their goals, their life became unbalanced. They spent too much time focusing on one or two areas of their life and not enough in others. While in pursuit of reaching the top in their careers, they may have neglected their health or neglected spending quality time with their loved ones. This can happen to anyone who does not take the time to evaluate their priorities in life. **Remember that life will give you what you truly desire, but make sure you have someone to share it with.**

> **"The size of your success is measured by the strength of your desire; the size of your dream; and how you handle disappointment along the way." Robert Kiyosaki**

Success in life will not be handed to you; you must challenge your limiting beliefs and take massive action towards your goals. There is nothing in life that can defeat you or deny you of success but yourself. No conditions can overtake you if you set life goals and focus consistently and persistently on your goals. Your own limiting thinking can defeat you; your lack of determination, indecisiveness, and lack of confidence in yourself can defeat you. Your success in life is up to you. **"According to thy faith be it unto thee." Matthew 9:29**

Most people continuously fail to achieve their desire in life because of their lack of faith in themselves. In the pursuit of their goals they did not believe enough in themselves; they focused too much on their life circumstances and gave up. Most are not willing to pay the price for what they want. When they are faced with opposition and get knocked down, they do not have the courage to get back up and go at it again. The instant you acknowledge that you are incapable of doing the thing you set out to do, or that some outside circumstances can block you from achieving your desires, you set up a barrier to your success that no amount of hard work can remove. Nothing is more detrimental to success than this sort of mental attitude.

We get in this life whatever we concentrate upon with our mind. Our success or failure is in our own hands. Prosperous people have prosperous attitudes. They are convinced that they can accomplish what they determine to accomplish, and that there is no reason why they cannot achieve all they envision. Prosperous people expect more good out of life; they expect to succeed without compromising their core values. People with the best attitude naturally rise to the top. **Think about your desire, talk about it, live it, breathe it, dream it, act it, saturate your life with it. You must believe that what you want is already yours**.

Where will you be five years from today in your life?

_____

_____

_____

_____

_____

_____

_____

_____

_____

_____

_____

_____

_____

_____

_____

_____

_____

_____

_____

_____

_____

_____

_____

_____

_____

If you have completed the exercise, I commend you for taking part in your success and also being coachable. You have to realize that you live in a world where you are the architect of your future. As the architect of your life you create what happens. You have got to accept 100% responsibility for where you are, who you are with, and what is happening to you.

You have got to decide what sort of life you want to lead. A success consciousness is a self-fulfilling reality. The more you start to think success, the more it will start to happen for you, the more you start to believe in it, the more you will be excited by it, the more your mind will get even more creative to come up with the next great idea, and the more you will go out there to find some new creative ways of doing things.

Key points:

- We get in this life whatever we concentrate upon with all of our mind.
- Success in life will not be handed to you.
- People with goals know exactly where they are going.
- You have got to decide what sort of life you want to lead.
- You are the architect of your future.

Built To Prosper "Desire" Quotes

"Those who restrain desire, do so because theirs is weak enough to be restrained."
William Blake

"The will to win, the desire to succeed, the urge to reach your full potential... these are the keys that will unlock the door to personal excellence."
Confucius

"In order to succeed, your desire for success should be greater than your fear of failure."
Anonymous

"It is for us to pray not for tasks equal to our powers, but for powers equal to our tasks, to go forward with a great desire forever beating at the door of our hearts as we travel toward our distant goal."
Helen Keller

"The desire of gold is not for gold. It is for the means of freedom and benefit."
Ralph Waldo Emerson

"Every person who wins in any undertaking must be willing to cut all sources of retreat. Only by doing so can one be sure of maintaining that state of mind known as a burning desire to win—essential to success."
Napoleon Hill

CHAPTER X

WHAT TO DO NOW? TAKE ACTION!

CHAPTER X
WHAT TO DO NOW? TAKE ACTION!

> "The success of the mission requires action and a strong work ethic – not a passive and irresponsible attitude. Purpose is the WHY and vision is the strategy." Hasheem Francis

Did you think I was going to leave you all puffed up feeling good with no action? Absolutely not. This is not that type of book; it is time to get to work. By reading this book and doing the exercises in each of the chapters, you should have an understanding of the principles of creating a prosperous life. If not, reread it again. As a matter of fact, read this book every three months, it will serve you well. Make sure you schedule it in your calendar. **Commit and take action!**

Have you heard the saying "knowledge is power"? Well it is not. *Applied* **knowledge is power**. Changing your life begins with information, but after that, it is all about what you do with that information that will change and improve your life. Having knowledge means being able to make choices. The only way to create change is to take action. I love this quote by Benjamin Franklin: **"He that waits upon fortune is never sure of a dinner."**

Once you set a goal for yourself, you must act immediately. Without action, you cannot expect to achieve anything different in your life. Too often people get stuck in the state of analysis paralysis and never reach the action stage. They have to have a meeting and then have a meeting about the meeting. You can create plans all day, but get moving. **Just identify the first physical action you need to take, and then do it**. For instance, if you have decided to have a better relationship with your spouse, go on a date and turn off the television. **Do not think about it, do not ponder, just do it!**

The time has come to go out and achieve your goals and live a life of prosperity. We have discussed the importance of your thoughts, words, attitude, and your belief in building a your desired life. **You have made the decision and I know you are committed to the process. You have come too far to turn back now.**

One of the principles of success is recognizing that a burning desire follows action. The momentum of continuous action fuels the desire, while procrastination kills it. **So act boldly, as if it is impossible to fail.** If you keep adding fuel to your desire, you will reach the point of knowing that you will never quit, and ultimate success will be nothing more than a matter of time.

> "Everything you want is out there waiting for you to ask. Everything you want also wants you. But you have to take action to get it." Jack Canfield

There are so many people who want to change or want more out of life than they are getting, but are not willing to take action in getting what they want. It is fine to talk about what you want and even to dream about it, but if you are not taking action, you will become frustrated in life. Plans and no action will keep you in the same position you are in. Many people make plans but they do not take the time to put them into action. Their favorite words are "I'm trying to." **The mindset of those who go out and achieve their goals is: either I do or I don't, there is no such thing as trying. I would rather watch a leader than listen to one any day. Action is the key.**

Whatever desires you may have, it will only be fulfilled if action is taken. First you must decide what you need to be content with your life and give yourself step-by-step aims. You would need to consider how much work you need to put in if you are ever to begin achieving those aims. Next, you should set a timeline for reaching your goals and create a plan highlighting how and when you will go about your tasks.

In order to turn the wheel of your consciousness and begin to walk in prosperity, you must do things you have never done before. As a leader, parent, business owner, or whatever is your current circumstances in life, it is your responsibility to change your conditions. You have the power to do it. Does your vision inspire you enough to take action?

To assist you on this journey, we will provide you with some action steps to take. Use them as a building block. Once you develop the proper habits, create an action plan that works best for you. **You have to do what works for you**. I will be your coach and guide you until you come into your own.

We are going to create some action steps for each area of your life. These steps are foundational for creating a prosperous life, but they will only work wonders for you if you **take action** and do them. Remember, all that you need is already inside you. **Your life becomes great only when you decide upon your major definite purpose and then work on it every single day**. The first area we are going to focus on is the spiritual area of life. This is the foundation and key for developing your life.

Spiritual Development: Got Faith?

"So God created man in his own image, in the image of God created he him; male and female created he them." Genesis 1:27

Before we begin, let me make this clear: Your relationship with God is personal and is between you and God, so this area of development in your life you must take seriously.

Spending time with God opens a realm in which He shares wisdom, knowledge, and understanding with you about circumstances you may be facing. In order to know God as the Creator, you must spend time with Him daily. He desires the best for our lives, so we must make time for Him in our daily activities. How you spend time and connect with God is up to you; this is your *personal* relationship with Him.

I found this to be the most important area of my life. I took notice of this when I began studying the Bible for myself. At first I thought the Bible was a book filled with do's and don'ts. Do not eat this, do not go there, do not say that, and love thy enemy. Wow that was a hard one. I truly believe the reason I thought this way was that I had someone else's opinion about what and who God is. In my earlier years, I never took the time to study the word of God for myself. I always relied on someone else's interpretation of it. I began to have some understanding is when I came across **1 John 4:8: "He that loveth not knoweth not God, for God is love."**

Once I found out that God is love, the next thing I had to do is seek what is true of **love.** And I found it in another passage, actually my wife Deborah did. We used it in our wedding and it has been our foundation scripture for our marriage:

"Love is patient, love is kind. It does not envy, it does not boast, it is not proud. It does not dishonor others, it is not self-seeking, it is not easily angered, it keeps no record of wrongs. Love does not delight in evil but rejoices with the truth. It always protects, always trusts, always hopes, always perseveres. Love never fails." 1 Corinthians 13:4-8

I really like **"Love never fails."** And you know what, since I began seeking God, He never failed me. Did I have some circumstances I did not think was fair? Yes, but I learned to look at things that are unfavorable as learning experiences. I believe in all the adversity I faced in life, God was shaping and molding me into a greater man. **Isaiah 64:8** says, **"But now, O LORD, thou art our father; we are the clay, and thou our potter; and we all are the work of thy hand."** It took time for me to understand this; it was a spiritual process and spiritual principles can only be discerned spiritually.

Spiritual growth is a process of shedding our wrong and unreal conceptions, thoughts, beliefs, and ideas, and becoming more conscious and aware of the God within us. French philosopher Teilhard de Chardin stated, **"We are not human beings having a spiritual experience. We are spiritual beings having a human experience."**

Having an understanding of our spiritual nature is of great importance for everyone, not only for people who seek a deeper connection to God or attend a religious service. Spiritual growth is the basis for a better and more harmonious life for everyone, a life free of tension, fear, and anxiety.

Spiritual growth is not a means of escaping from responsibilities, behaving strangely, and becoming an impractical person. It is a method of growing and becoming a stronger, happier, and more responsible person. A balanced life requires that we take care not only of the necessities of the body, feelings, and mind, but also of the spirit, and this is the role of spiritual growth.

Spiritual Development Action Steps:

- If you have a library card, check out an uplifting spiritual book. What book you choose is up to you. Take some time each morning to seek and find the meaning of having a relationship with God.
- Be grateful for what you currently have in your life. Write five things you are grateful for each night before you go to bed. Gratitude draws you closer to God.
- Learn to quiet your mind through concentration exercises and meditation. Focus on what is on the inside of you and try to find out what is it that makes you feel alive.

Personal Development: Got A Growth Plan?

> **"If you don't design your own life plan, chances are you will fall into someone else's plan. And guess what they have planned for you? Not much." Jim Rohn**

The next area we are going to focus on is personal development. Success is an ongoing process. Development does not stop after this book. This is just the beginning and there is so much more to learn; you must be a lifelong learner. Development takes time and involves a range of experiences, guidance, and training. **Your goal is to develop the skills that support the competencies needed to succeed in life**.

Having a personal development plan is a wise investment in yourself. The reason it is called personal development is that the plan is personal to you. When you make your own personal development plan, it can provide you with a self-reflection. One of the objectives of this endeavor is assessing your capabilities, including your skills, personal strengths, and knowledge. You can develop a plan that focuses on your strengths or weakness.

When I started developing myself I became amazed at all the information and resources that were available. All the solutions to life circumstances were in books, all I had to do was find the book and apply the principles to get the results I desired. The problem was in the **consistent application of the principles**. I would read book after book and not see any results. I would hear someone say a certain book changed their life and I ran out and got that book. I was addicted to the personal development process. My growth plan was not focused, at first I never took the time out to apply the principles in many of these books.

Then something happened. I was at an event and heard several speakers, who were successful businessmen and women, say Napoleon Hill's *Think and Grow Rich* helped change their life. That was not my first time hearing someone say that book changed their life. At that point I had already read *Think and Grow Rich* and I was not rich then. I got to a point in my life where I said enough is enough. I will no longer play the victim, or continue down the path of missed opportunities. I got tired of my life going around and around in circles, only to end up with nothing. I started to ask myself; "Why are they successful, what do they have that I do not have? And why is my life like this? What do I need to do to get better results?"

I wanted more, so I began my journey on being a great student of life, so I could be an outstanding teacher of living.

In life, you must plan for personal development. The first step is to make a true analysis of "Where am I today?" and "Where do I want to go?" Second, you must identify resources available to help you get there. Third, you must implement a plan that can lead to successful development. All of the successful people I know made a habit of creating a developmental plan. Remember earlier I said my mentor told me "success leaves clues." He also said **"If you want what successful people have, you have to read what successful people read, and do what successful people do."**

Personal Development Action Steps:

- Apply for a library card, it is free. If you have one, then great. The library is going to become your second home. **Be a lifelong learner.**

- Go to the library and check out one of the books we have in the recommended reading list in the back of this book. No particular order; just select one you may be interested in. Most importantly decide, then **pick the book up and read it.**

- **Turn your vehicle into Drive Time University.** Instead of being bombarded with advertising and constant negative news, listen to audio programs that inspire you. Some of the books in the recommended reading list are in audio format as well.

- Take a break from the television for a week. This may be difficult if you are addicted to the TV and I hope it is difficult for you to do. **I want you to be uncomfortable.** Living in the comfort zone is a sure fire way to ensure your own misery.

- Create a personal journal. Write down your thoughts. You will be creating your blueprint for success.

Health Plan: Did You Eat Your Broccoli?

"The first wealth is health." Ralph Waldo Emerson

What is the point of wealth without health? My wife Deborah once told me, "Without health, you will not enjoy your wealth." I reflected on what she said and I got my act together fast. I did not want someone else enjoying the fruits of my labor. What purpose is there in having all the wealth you desire but not having the health to enjoy it? Taking control of your health is of utmost importance because your body and mind are your most valuable assets and determine your well being. You can create a healthy lifestyle by making conscious choices. The components of healthy living also include practicing healthy habits, like exercising. Taking control of your health will result in more energy, mental alertness, enthusiasm, and creativity.

Getting the proper and adequate nutrition is important. Your body requires fresh food and plenty of water. Fresh fruits and vegetables provide nutrients and enzymes. I make no claims to be a health specialist, I just took the time to read and learn about my health. I give my wife all the credit for helping me develop the habit of eating more fruits and vegetables. She put it on the plate and I ate. If you have been married for a while you know, if the wife took the time to cook, you better take the time to eat. **A healthy lifestyle also comprises of having a positive mental attitude to enable you to remain optimistic and grateful**.

Regardless of your time pressures, you need to take a break and practice the habit of taking leisure time for rest and recreation. Make it a daily habit to sit quietly and relax your body and feel calm inside. I will be honest, this is difficult for me. I am like the energizer bunny; I keep going and going and going. Vacations with me were like being in a marathon; I would run around and try to do every activity before the vacation was over. My wife Deborah, on the other hand, would just take her precious time, relax, and enjoy the vacation. She would be refreshed and I would be exhausted after it was over. My wife had to step in and had a nice little talk with me. She said, **"If you want to be around long enough to see your grandchildren, you better learn how relax."** That woman sure does love me! As a matter of fact, I think I should call my wife and have her write this section of the book. I still struggle with relaxing, although I am getting better. I am not where I used to be. I am learning to go with the flow.

Health Action Steps:

- Drink more water. Develop the habit of drinking more water than flavored drinks. Drink at least ½ your body weight in water per day.

- Exercise for twenty minutes daily. It can either be walking, running, or weight lifting or an exercise you enjoy. Be consistent.

- Eat more fruits and vegetables. Eating healthy is important. There are some great nutrition books you can pick up from the library.

- Take time to relax. Take twenty minutes daily to yourself where you can focus on breathing and calming all the noise in your mind.

- Get rest, get rest, get rest. Give your body the proper rest it needs. Believe me, I know what can be done to a body that has not received proper rest.

- Give your body the essentials it needs for healthy living with whole food supplements. Make sure you research the company and the product before you use it.

Relationship Building: Who Is In Your Network?

"If we are together nothing is impossible. If we are divided all will fail." Winston Churchill

A strong, healthy relationship can be one of the best supports in your life. Good relationships improve your life in all aspects, strengthening your health, mind, and connection with others. However, it can also be one of the greatest drains if the relationship is not working. **Relationships are an investment. The more you put in, the more you get back.** Love and relationships take work, commitment, a willingness to adapt, and change through life as a team.

It is important that you develop the right relationships. When most people talk about relationships, they usually say they want a 50-50 relationship. Why would you want to give only half of your potential? **For a relationship to be meaningful, you must give 100%.**

Building and maintaining a quality relationship takes time. When people are asked, "What is one of the most important ingredients in a relationship?" communication is always at the top of the list, yet we are rarely taught how to communicate effectively. My mentor once shared with me an insight that I am forever grateful for: "God gave us one mouth and two ears for a reason. We need to learn how to talk less and listen more." Have you noticed that when you are with people who are great listeners they seem to have a magnetism about them? You just seem to be drawn to them. On the other hand, when you are in the presence of the infamous talkers, you feel mentally drained afterwards. When you see the infamous talkers you literally want to run in the opposite direction. In a relationship, communication is about sharing, which consists of each person being able to express him or herself freely without the opposite party placing judgment. When you know how to give and receive you can develop some wonderful lifelong relationships.

You could have all the money in the world, but if you do not have someone special to share it with, it would be senseless. Life could be lonely without good people to experience it with. I just realized something: Benjamin Franklin, Andrew Jackson, or George Washington (money) never hugged me in the middle of the night. It would be scary if they did, but you know what I mean.

❖ **Quality Relationships + Money = Wonderful Experiences**
❖ **Money – Quality Relationships = Lonely Life**
❖ **Quality Relationships – Money = A Donation-Based Life**

"The poor is hated even of his own neighbor: but the rich hath many friends." **Proverbs 14:20**

"Wealth maketh many friends; but the poor is separated from his neighbor." **Proverbs 19:4**

So how do you build quality relationships? First you must set the example. Ralph Waldo Emerson stated, **"The only way to have a friend is to be a friend."** If you do not know what it means to be a friend, in the Circle of Trust chapter, we did an exercise listing the ten qualities you value in a relationship. Take those qualities and exemplify them. Next you must respect others. In order to get respect, you must first show respect.

A major stumbling block in any relationship is settling disagreements. When you are wrong, learn to admit your mistakes. This could be a hard one, because we live in a world where everyone wants to be right. If we learn to communicate effectively with others and are willing to share our true feelings and respect other people's feelings, many benefits will await us as we learn to build relationships with one another.

Relationships Action Steps:

- Make a list of all the successful people you know personally who have great relationships, and take each one of them to lunch individually. Ask them questions about how they developed their relationships. Make this a lunch-and-learn.
- Attend one networking event each month. Make a new contact and build a relationship.
- Treat everyone you meet with respect, no matter who they are.
- Learn to be a great listener.

Business/Career Development: Mind Your Business

> "Good business leaders create a vision, articulate the vision, passionately own the vision, and relentlessly drive it to completion." Jack Welch

In this area we are going to focus on developing and maintaining a business. You may be thinking, "I do not want to be a business owner, I would rather work for someone." The truth is, even if you get a job or build a career, you would still need to treat it as a business. Some of the principles we discuss in this section could be applied to a career as well. It takes courage and commitment to be a business owner, but there are so many benefits and risks in owning a business.

Let us look at some of the positives of entrepreneurship:

You have control over your salary. You determine how much you are worth.

- You control your time – You decide how many hours you are going to work.
- You are in charge of your own destiny. You make the decisions; no one can tell you when you can go to the bathroom or on vacation. You can promote yourself anytime.
- You have options. You can decide how many employees you want to hire.
- You can become a community builder. Your business can have a positive effect on the community.

Now are you ready to start your business? Here are some of the most important questions you must ask before you journey into entrepreneurship:

Would my product or service add value to the market? Let us be honest: the startup phase in starting a business is time-consuming. You will find yourself questioning whether you have made the right decision, especially when the hours are long and the initial profits (if any) are lean. Starting a company from the ground up is no get-rich-quick thing. As the business owner, you are also the number one salesperson for your organization. Your enthusiasm for your product or service—whether it is health products or international business consulting—is often the difference that brings purchasing customers, lands deals, and attracts investors. It is unwise to start down the path of entrepreneurship unless you have a zeal that will get you through rough patches and keep you interested long after the initial enthusiasm has faded.

Do I have a business plan? A business plan provides an outline of the vision, overview, and goals of your new business. It will help you stay on track while you build your business; and referring back to this plan will re-direct focus to your original intentions for creating the business. This plan is not only for you to view, but investors that will evaluate your business strategy will also read it.

What is my IQ (I Quit) level? Whether it is resigning from your day job or opening a storefront office, nothing about starting a business is for the faint of heart. This is not for the employee-minded or those looking for a steady paycheck. Business consultant Deborah Francis tells aspiring entrepreneurs they have to **"Take action, and be willing to jump off the cliff and figure out how to fly on the way down."** There is no guarantee of success, or even a steady paycheck. If you are risk-averse, entrepreneurship is probably not the right path for you. Stick with your day job.

Am I an effective decision maker? No one else is going to make decisions for you when you own your own business. You can not call mommy. Consider how you might handle these early decisions: Do I incorporate? Do I use a corporate tax ID or my social security number? Do I use my hard earned savings or get a loan? Do I work from home or do I purchase office space? Do I hire employees? How much do I invest in marketing? Keep in mind that the decision-making process only gets more complicated as time goes on, once you have employees or clients depending on you. The choices you make can lead to success or failure, so you must feel confident in your ability to make the right call.

Am I willing to be the CEO, Manager, and Janitor? While a corporate employee focuses on a special skill or role within the larger corporation, a business owner must contribute everything to the business. Startup entrepreneurs in particular must be versatile and play a number of roles, from chief salesperson, to bookkeeper, to head marketer, and bill collector. If juggling many roles does not suit you, entrepreneurship probably will not either.

Am I willing to go the distance? Working six days a week, not on a 9-to-5 schedule, abandoning old hobbies and interests, and not spending quality time with your loved ones can quickly lead to doubts and fears in the midst of a business's initial startup. If you do not have the discipline and focus, the beginning stages of building your business can lead to failure. This is what happens to many first time entrepreneurs. If you are able to develop and maintain good habits that create a balance between your life and your business, such as not working on certain days, making time for hobbies such as reading, exercising, and going on weekly dates with your spouse, life as an entrepreneur can be rewarding, and most importantly, fun.

Excuse me, business owner: Got cash flow? Proper management of the cash flow in your business will determine the long-term success of your company. **A business that has no cash flow is considered a hobby, and we all know hobbies cost money.** If you are a business owner and there is a cash flow issue, you will need to do a complete analysis of your business model from the top down.

Do you have a blueprint for success for your business? Got cash? Cash is king in business. When cash is flowing in a business, it gives the business an opportunity for expansion, such as hiring new team members to take the business to the next level, or maybe expanding the business to an international market. Many first-time business owners fail at properly managing cash flow. Instead of reinvesting back into their business, they take the cash and spend it on personal use. I have seen this happen many times with people who make that transition from being an employee to an entrepreneur. They are so used to having a paycheck coming in on a consistent basis that when their business starts to earn revenue, they eat the first fruits from the tree instead of planting the seeds to grow a bigger tree.

Cash flow management is essential for businesses that succeed. Cash flow is one of the key elements to taking your business to the next level. A business that does earn and manage its revenue can cause a great deal of stress to first time business owners. **With most startup businesses, it may take some time before the business starts to generate cash flow, and that is okay.** But you must determine how much time you are willing to invest in a business that is not generating cash flow. Is your team willing to stick and stay? If you are interested in laying a foundation for a profitable business currently and into the future, you must inspect what you expect. Put it all in writing so you can have it before you. If you need help analyzing the numbers, seek professional counsel from someone who has experience in running a successful business. The objective for your business is to track your income and expenses so that you put your business in a position to prosper. And you do want to prosper, correct?

You must realize that your business is an asset that will thrive when you analyze where your business is currently and then move into the mode of creating cash flow projection. Savvy business owners know how to create and come within the constraints of a cash flow analysis based on a weekly, monthly, and yearly projection. When you have been in business for a few years, a review of your company's cash flow patterns will help you to evaluate any areas that need to be amplified so your business can continue to grow.

Business/Career Action Steps:

- Decide if you are going to be an employee or an entrepreneur, then develop a roadmap for your job or business success.
- Find a mentor who is currently successful in business or area you are looking to develop a career in and invite them out to lunch. You pay. **Lunch and learn!**
- Create a list of things you are good at and could potentially turn into a business. Research the internet and see if there are businesses like this.
- Seek the advice of leaders in your industry, business bankers, and business financial planners that have attained high levels of success and are willing to empower you to reach your goals.

Financial Plan: Cash or Credit?

> **"Rule No. 1: Never lose money. Rule No. 2: Never forget rule No. 1." Warren Buffett**

You must take responsibility for your financial state. It is going to take money to live a prosperous life. Eating healthy is going require money, having the experiences that support meaningful relationships requires money, starting a business requires money. Prosperity does not run on credit. **If you are going to operate in this world, you are going to need money.**

Most people think earning a large six- or seven-figure income is the key to financial freedom, but it is not. I know many people who earn a six- or seven-figure income, but they spend every dime of it and end up spending more than they earn by trying to keep up with the Joneses. They smell good and look good, but they are broke. You know how I know this? Because I once lived in that world. Years ago when I started making some real money, I did not have the financial discipline or mindset to accompany the money. You could say I was really out of control. I took exotic trips, I dined at the most expensive restaurants, and I brought new shoes and clothes like I was crazy. Did I think about saving or put any money aside for investing or save for a rainy day? Oh no, it was not raining, it was sunny outside everyday when I had money. Did I make some mistakes? Absolutely.

I have learned that if you try to live up to other people's financial standards of what automobile you should drive, where you should live, and what you should wear, you could end up in a great deal of trouble. And I was in trouble. I over-leveraged myself with debt obligations. At one point I owed everyone and their mother. I got sick and tired of living that way; I was trying to impress people with money I did not have. I had many sleepless nights because I knew I could do better financially and never really liked owing money to anyone. I felt my bad money habits were a flaw on my character. I was not the type of person to hide from my creditors. I heard about people doing this but I was not buying into it. I wanted to be responsible; they loaned me the money and as a responsible person my goal was to pay it back no matter the circumstances. When the creditors would call, I would simply say, "I did not have the money at that time but as soon as I got it, you would get your money." And you know what, I got treated with respect. I took responsibility for the financial decisions I made. From that moment on, I began to postpone the pleasures of the moment such as buying things on credit and spending every dime. I focused on wealth building, by learning what successful people were doing with their wealth. I also began reading financial journals. **You could say I studied myself out of a broke mentality into a wealth mentality**. I had plenty of help as well. Thank God for my mentors. They say "when the student is ready, the teacher will appear."

Do I have any regrets about how I used my money? Absolutely...Not, it was a learning experience. I would have never gained this insight if I had not gone through that experience. Now, I am free and I do not allow other people's opinion of me to determine what I desire in life. You will never be able to take charge of your life or really be free to be who you want to be until you to learn to accept full responsibility for your life right now. **One of the most important things in life is having your financial house in order.**

When you talk to financially successful people, they know how much they are worth, how much they earn on a monthly and/or annual basis, how much they pay in taxes, and they know exactly how much they are putting away towards their family legacy. They are thoughtful regarding every aspect of their financial lives. As a result, they are never broke. They always have money in the bank. They enjoy a far higher standard of living than the average person. Your goal is to join the financial elite by thinking and acting the way they do.

It is time to get your financial house in order. To do this, you will need to have a financial tracking sheet or book where you can list all of your outstanding debt, monthly expenses, and income.

Financial Action Steps:

- Get a financial journal. This will help you keep track of your daily, monthly, and yearly expenses.
- Track your weekly, biweekly, and monthly income.
- Gather all your bills and write what your monthly expenses are.
- If you have credit card debt or any other debt, know the interest rate you are paying.
- Find a financial professional who is "successful with their finances" and take them out to lunch, you pay. **Lunch and learn!**

Start now! Do not procrastinate. Without implementing any of the action steps that you have mapped out for yourself, this book simply becomes an exercise in reading. In order to gain the full benefits this valuable book has to offer, make the decision here and now that you will act upon the strategies, and you will achieve the kind of results in your life that you never thought possible. I want to see you wealthy!

90 Day Action Plan:

Create a list of goals you would like to achieve in the next 90 days. Write your goals in the present tense, as though 90 days have passed and each of them has already been attained. Use the words, "I am, I earn, I drive, I have, I achieved, etc." Whenever you use the word "I" with regard to yourself, you program your subconscious mind to go to work on your goal all day long.

Assignment:

Purchase a recorder if you do not have one. I want you to record yourself speaking positive affirmations to yourself and listen to them twice daily: when you first wake up and just before you go to sleep. Your voice is the most powerful voice to your subconscious mind. Feed your mind with words that strengthen you and move you to act with passion.

The mechanics that make affirmations powerful are repetition, emotions, persistence and belief. You must feel what it would be like when the desire you are affirming is fulfilled or your needs met. Every time you have a need and it is met, a certain feeling is produced in you. You need to evoke that same feeling when you state your affirmation.

Personalize your affirmations. They must resonate with you and feel right for you. The stronger your connection with the affirmation, the deeper the impression it makes on your mind, and the sooner you will experience positive results.

Affirmations:

- I now claim my birthright to prosperity.

- I walk by faith, not by sight.

- I am love, I give love, and I am loved.

- There is more than enough for me and everyone to live prosperously.

- I fully open myself up to receive prosperity from the universe.

- I choose to live prosperously and share my abundance with others.

- I am not given a spirit of fear, but of love, and of power, and of a sound mind.

- I choose to live with confidence, peace, happiness, and kindness.

- I choose to give generously.

- I am open and willing, so I receive joyously.

- I am blessed to be rich; money comes to me from all directions.

- I am thankful and content today.

- Money is my employee and is here to serve me.

- I am always expecting the best for myself.

- I make wise investment choices that bring more and more money to invest.

- I allow unlimited prosperity to flow to me everyday.

- I tithe 10% of all income I receive.

- Money comes easily and effortlessly. I am a good receiver.

- I love to share and it brings me joy.

- I think and speak positively. I focus on what is good. I refuse to fear or dwell on the negative.

- I can accomplish anything I set my mind on.

- I delight in You, Lord, and You give me the desires of my heart.

- God provides and supplies all needs for me and all humanity.

- I am grateful for all the abundance I receive and the lifestyle I live.

- I give thanks for ever increasing health, youth, and beauty.

- I am responsible for my own attitude.

- I expect lavish abundance every day in every way in my life and affairs.

- Wealth and abundance come to me naturally!

- This is God's day, a good day. I pronounce this day and all of its activities good!

- Every day I am increasing my wealth.

- I see every opportunity that comes my way.

Built To Prosper "Action" Quotes:

"There are risks and costs to action. But they are far less than the long range risks of comfortable inaction."
John F. Kennedy

"The chief condition on which life, health, and vigor depend is action. It is by action that an organism develops its faculties, increases its energy, and attains the fulfillment of its destiny."
Colin Powell

"Do you want to know who you are? Don't ask. Act! Action will delineate and define you."
Thomas Jefferson

"A real decision is measured by the fact that you've taken a new action. If there's no action, you haven't truly decided."
Tony Robbins

"An ounce of action is worth a ton of theory."
Ralph Waldo Emerson

"Action is a great restorer and builder of confidence. Inaction is not only the result, but the cause, of fear. Perhaps the action you take will be successful; perhaps different action or adjustments will have to follow. But any action is better than no action at all."
Norman Vincent Peale

"Inaction breeds doubt and fear. Action breeds confidence and courage. If you want to conquer fear, do not sit home and think about it. Go out and get busy."
Dale Carnegie

The Last Word...

I have poured my heart and soul into each of the pages sharing the principles of self mastery, and it all begins with making the decision to live more abundantly.

Now the only thing standing between you and success is your application of the principles bestowed within this book and allowing them time to move you forward!

On your journey, make sure you take time to celebrate every little success. Even if you are the only one who notices it.

I believe in you. I believe you have it within you to accomplish anything your heart desires. You will need to stay focused and disciplined to do it. If you came this far, there is no turning back.

Hasheem Francis
Co-Founder, CEO
Built To Prosper Companies
www.BuiltToProsperCompanies.com
info@BuiltToProsperCompanies.com

BIBLIOGRAPHY

Francis, Deborah and Francis, Hasheem. **CASHOLOGY The Science of Living A Cash Only Life.** Plymouth, FL.: BTP Publishing Group, 2010.

Baines, John. **The Secret Science.** John Baines Institute, 1994

Francis, Deborah. **The Joy of Healthy Living, Without Your Health You Cannot Enjoy Your Wealth**. Plymouth, FL.: The Joy of Healthy Living, LLC , 2011.

Haanel, Charles. F. **The Master Key System**. St. Louis: Psychology Publishing, 1916

Hill, Napoleon. **Think and Grow Rich**. New York, NY: Penguin, 2008.

Thompson, Leroy, Dr. **Money Cometh: To The Body of Christ**. Darrow, LA: Ever Increasing Word Ministries , 1999.

Thompson, Leroy, Dr. **I'll Never Be Broke Another Day in My Life**. Darrow, LA: Ever Increasing Word Ministries, 2001.

Wattles, Wallace. D. **The Science Of Getting Rich**. New York: Elizabeth Towne Company, 1910.

Wattles, Wallace. D. **The Science Of Being Well**. New York: Elizabeth Towne Company, 1910.

ABOUT THE AUTHOR
Hasheem Francis

Hasheem Francis is the Co-founder & Chairman of Built To Prosper Companies. Hasheem Francis is an entrepreneur, investor, bestselling author, keynote speaker, recognized industry thought leader, and an expert on executive business and leadership development.

With two decades of entrepreneurial and leadership experience, Hasheem Francis is a leadership consultant and advisor to CEOs, business leaders, corporate executives and community leaders across the country. His vast expertise in dealing with business change, along with his strong financial investment background and leadership development skills, enables him to provide unique and unparalleled counsel to a diverse range of industry professionals. Hasheem has served as a founder, partner, CEO, CFO, and leadership consultant for a diverse range of entrepreneurial and mature companies. His expression of faithfulness and determination continues to be an inspirational success for countless others who bear witness to the example that he personifies as a man of purpose.

BUILT TO PROSPER
MENTORING
BUSINESS AND LEADERSHIP DEVELOPMENT

RECOMMENDED
READING LIST

BUILT TO PROSPER MENTORING RECOMMENDED READING LIST:

Personal Development

1. *The Slight Edge* – Jeff Olson
2. *A Fortune to Share* – Paul J. Meyer
3. *Awaken the Giant Within* – Anthony Robbins
4. *Pathway to Platinum* – Brian Curruthers
5. *The Millionaire Mind* – Thomas Stanley
6. *Twelve Pillars* – Chris Widner & Jim Rohn
7. *How to Win Friends and Influence People* – Dale Carnegie
8. *Lead the Field* – Earl Nightingale
9. *The Strangest Secret* – Earl Nightingale
10. *The Power of the Subconscious Mind* – Dr. Joseph Murphy
11. *The Art of Influence* – Chris Widener
12. *The Magic of Believing* – Claude Bristol
13. *The Science of Mind* – Ernest Holmes
14. *Finding the Magnetic Leader Within* – Nick Nicholas
15. *Way of the Peaceful Warrior* – Dan Millman
16. *The Alchemist* – Paulo Coelho
17. *The Power of Positive Thinking* – Norman Vincent Peale
18. *The Success Principle* – Jack Canfield
19. *The Success System That Never Fails* – Clement Stone
20. *Psycho-Cybernetics* – Maxwell Maltz
21. *How Successful People Think* – John Maxwell
22. *Above Life's Turmoil* – James Allen
23. *How to Grow Success* – Elizabeth Towne
24. *Compound Effect* – Darren Hardy
25. *Science of Being Great* – Wallace D. Wattles

BUILT TO PROSPER
——————MENTORING——————
BUSINESS AND LEADERSHIP DEVELOPMENT

Spiritual Life

1. *The Holy Bible*
2. *The Laws of Thinking* – Bishop E. Bernard Jordan
3. *Prayer of Jabez* – Bruce Wilkerson
4. *God's Creative Power* – Charles Capp
5. *Financial Prosperity* – Kenneth Copeland
6. *The Marked Bible* – Charles L. Taylor
7. *Enemy Access Denied* – John Bevere
8. *The Power of Praying Together* – Stormie Omartian
9. *Every Man's Battle* – Stephen Arterburn
10. *The Prideful Soul's Guide To Humility* – Michael Fontenot & Thomas Jones
11. *The Ultimate Gift* – Jim Stovall
12. *Some Sat in Darkness* – Mike Leatherwood
13. *Life on the High Wire* – Martin Camp
14. *The Greatest Salesman in the World* – Og Mandino
15. *Become a Better You* – Joel Osteen
16. *The Science of Love* – John Baine
17. *24 Keys that Bring Complete Success* – Paul J. Meyer
18. *Loose that Man & Let Him Go* – T.D Jakes
19. *How to find Your Wealthy Place* – Dr. Leroy Thompson
20. *Secret Ingredients for Spiritual Growth* – Dr. Robert Kennedy
21. *Framing Your World* – Dr. Leroy Thompson
22. *Battlefield of The Mind* – Joyce Meyer
23. *8 Steps to Create the Life You Want* – Creflo Dollar
24. *You Were Born For This* – Bruce Wilkinson
25. *The Everyday Visionary* – Jesse Duplantis

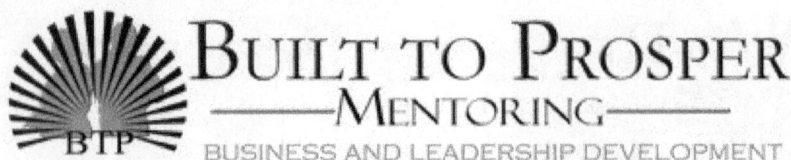

BUILT TO PROSPER
——MENTORING——
BUSINESS AND LEADERSHIP DEVELOPMENT

Wealth

1. *I'll Never BeBroke Another Day in My Life* – Dr. Leroy Thompson
2. *You Were Born Rich* – Bob Proctor
3. *Commander of Covenant Wealth* – Dr. Leroy Thompson
4. *Money Cometh* – Dr. Leroy Thompson
5. *Protecting Your #1 Assets* – Michael Lechter
6. *Dynamic Laws of Prosperity* – Catherine Ponder
7. *Cashology Academy* – Deborah Francis & Hasheem Francis
8. *The Wealth Magnet* – Dr. Dolf De Roos
9. *Why We Want You Rich* – Donald Trump & Robert Kiyosaki
10. *Rich Dad Poor Dad* – Robert Kiyosaki
11. *Think and Grow Rich* – Napoleon Hill
12. *The Secret to Attracting Money* – Dr. Joe Vital
13. *The Richest Man in Babylon* – George S. Clason
14. *Cashflow Quadrants* – Robert Kiyosaki
15. *The Master of Money* – Rev Ike
16. *Think Like a Billionaire* – Scot Anderson
17. *Multiple Streams of Income* – Robert Allen
18. *21 Distinctions of Wealth* – Peggy McColl
19. *Million Dollar Mindset* – James Arthur Ray
20. *Billionaire Secrets to Success* – Bill Bartmann
21. *Secrets of the Millionaire Mind* – T. Harv Eker
22. *Prosperity* – Charles Filmore
23. *The Way to Wealth* – Benjamin Franklin

BUILT TO PROSPER
——MENTORING——
BUSINESS AND LEADERSHIP DEVELOPMENT

Leadership

1. *The Leadership Bible* – John C. Maxwell
2. *The Seven Habits of Highly Effective People* – Stephen R. Covey
3. *Developing the Leader within You* – John C. Maxwell
4. *Lincoln on Leadership* – Donald Phillips
5. *Become the Leader You Were Meant to Be* – Paul J. Meyer
6. *Man of Steel & Velvet* – Aubrey Andelin
7. *Undeniable Confidence* – Hasheem Francis & Deborah Francis
8. *The 21 Irrefutable Laws of Leadership* – John C. Maxwell
9. *The Leadership Pill* – Ken Blanchard
10. *Built to Prosper* – Hasheem Francis
11. *Awaken The Giant Within* – Tony Robbins
12. *Who Moved My Cheese* – Spencer Johnson
13. *Corps Values* – Zell Miller
14. *Living at the Summit* – Dr. Tom Hill with John & Elizabeth Gardner
15. *The Art of Leadership* – J. Donald Walters
16. *The Pre Paid Legal Story* – Harland Stonecipher
17. *How to Build a Large Organization* – Paul J. Meyer
18. *Extreme Dreams Depend on Teams* – Pat Williams
19. *A Leader in the Making* – Joyce Meyer
20. *Message of a Master* – John McDonald
21. *TNT The Power Within You* – Claude Bristol
22. *The Leadership Challenge* – James Kouzes
23. *The Five Dysfunctions of a Team* – Patrick Lencioni
24. *Good to Great* – Jim Collins

Marriage & Family

1. *The Holy Bible*
2. *The Power of a Praying Wife* – Stormie Omartian
3. *Friends & Lovers* – Sam & Geri Laing
4. *The Power of Praying Together* – Stormie Omartian
5. *Love Your Husband* – Gloria Baird
6. *Smart Couples Finish Rich* – David Bach
7. *Every Man's Battle* – Stephen Arterburn
8. *Love Dare* – Stephen Kendrick
9. *The Five Love Languages, Men's Edition* – Steve Shores
10. *The Purpose Driven Life* – Rick Warren
11. *The Science of Love* – John Baine
12. *The Five Languages of Love* – Gary D. Chapman
13. *You Can Heal Your Life* – Louise Hay
14. *Wake Up The Mighty Men* – Darlene Bishop
15. *Courtship After Marriage* – Zig Ziglar
16. *Family Promises* – Kenneth Copeland
17. *The Power of a Praying Husband* – Stormie Omartian
18. *The Discipline Book* – Dr. Sears
19. *The Man in the Mirror* – Patrick Morley
20. *The Power of a Praying Parent* – Stormie Omartian
21. *Grooming the Next Generation* – Dani Johnson
22. *The Power of Prayer to Change Your Marriage* – Stormie Omartian
23. *How to Put Your Family Under the Anointing* – Dr. Leroy Thompson

Built to Prosper
——Mentoring——
BUSINESS AND LEADERSHIP DEVELOPMENT

Health

1. *The Seven Pillars of Health* – Dr. Don Colbert
2. *The Science of Being Well* – Wallace D. Wattles
3. *Natural Health, Natural Medicine* – Andrew Weil
4. *Perfect Health* – Deepak Chopra, M.D.
5. *Eat This and Live* – Dr. Don Colbert
6. *Live In The Divine Health* – Dr. Don Colbert
7. *What You Don't Know May Be Killing You* – Dr. Don Colbert
8. *Toxic Relief* – Dr. Don Colbert
9. *Platinum Workout* – LL Cool J
10. *Mind/Body Nutrition* – Marc David
11. *The Flex Brain Method* – Nightingale Learning System
12. *I Can Do This Diet* – Dr. Don Colbert
13. *Look Great, Feel Great* – Joyce Meyers
14. *Eat to Live* – Joel Fuhrman
15. *Change Your Habits, Change Your Life* – Danna Demetre
16. *Live Long, Finish Strong* – Gloria Copeland
17. *Billy's Ultimate Bootcamp* – Billy Blanks
18. *The Everything Family Nutrition Book* – Leslie Bilderback
19. *Prime Time Health* – William Sears, M.D.
20. *The Joy of Healthy Living* – Deborah Francis

This is by no means a complete list of valuable resources for health. Criteria for picking appropriate literature include language quality and quality of principles taught within the book.

Notes

_____

_____

_____

_____

_____

_____

_____

_____

_____

_____

_____

_____

_____

_____

_____

_____

Notes

Notes

Notes

www.ingramcontent.com/pod-product-compliance
Lightning Source LLC
Chambersburg PA
CBHW031250090426
42742CB00007B/396